Breaking the Spell of Dharma and Other Essays

ii ❧

Breaking the Spell of Dharma
and Other Essays

SECOND EDITION, REVISED AND UPDATED

Meera Nanda

Second Edition March 2007
copyright©Three Essays, 2007

ISBN 978-81-88789-52-8

Three Essays
COLLECTIVE

B-957 Palam Vihar, GURGAON (Haryana) 122 017 India
Phone: +91 98681 26587, +91 98683 44843
info@threeessays.com   Website: www.threeessays.com
Printed and bound at Glorious Printers, New Delhi

Contents

Acknowledgements

Defending the Enlightenment is not the surest way to win friends and influence people in the postmodern academia, especially in the United States where these essays were written. That is why the friends I did win over and who, in turn, influenced me deserve special words of gratitude.

I am enormously grateful to those rare Indian intellectuals working in the United States who extended a hand of friendship. I cannot thank Sanjib Baruah enough for his encouragement and support. Harsh Kapoor, Darshan Perusek and Samir Chopra gave words of encouragement when I needed them the most. My old friends, Puran and Nandita Mongia, were always a source of support.

My old and new-found friends from South Asia read my work and sent me their feedback. I found my communications with Achin Vanaik, Bipan Chandra, K.N. Panikkar, Pervez Hoodbhoy, T. Jayaraman, Maithreyi Krishnaraj, Gopal Guru and Sharmila Rege most enlightening. My critics Gita Chadha and Sundar Sarukkai deserve a special word of thanks for making me think harder. My fellow rationalist, Dr. Visvanathan, shared his wonderful essays on Indian medicine with me.

Thanks are due also to Krishna Raj, the editor of the *Economic and Political Weekly*. He has always encouraged me to submit my essays to EPW and has been most generous in giving me space.

Alan Sokal and his wonderful wife, Marina Papa, provided intellectual kinship and friendship. I am also grateful to Noretta Koertege, Cassandra Pinnick, James Maffie, Susan Haack, Philip Kitcher, Stephen Bronner, Irene Gendzier – they have been excellent teachers and comrades. Langdon Winner, my dissertation advisor and friend, helped me navigate the tricky waters of academia. Daphne Patai and Martin Lewis have been steadfast in their friendship.

This collection of essays owes its existence to Asad Zaidi and Nalini Taneja. They were kind enough to include my work in the series of readings Three Essays Collective is publishing.

Last but not the least, I appreciate the love and support of Ravi Rajamani, my partner, and Jaya, our daughter. They have made it all possible.

Preface to the New Edition

It brings me great pleasure to see a new edition of my book, *Breaking the Spell of Dharma.*

The plea the book made for breaking ourselves free from the spell of the gods is as valid and urgent today as it was when it first appeared nearly five years ago.

India has seen an intensification of neo-liberal globalization in recent years. Globalization is proving to be good for the gods. The growing Indian middle class is shopping for the right deities and the right gurus to bless their growing aspirations and appetites, while the poor left behind in the dust have no one else but God to turn to. As a result, religious rituals are getting more ostentatious, neighborhood temples are getting gentrified, and new gurus are doing roaring business while entirely new gods and traditions are being invented.

But more ominously, people are not only praying more often and more openly, they are praying more self-consciously, as if to declare to the world their identities as Hindus, Muslims, Christians, Sikhs or others. Even though Hindu nationalist parties have lost the reins of the government at the center, the imposition of Hindu symbols, rituals and practices on non-Hindu minorities has not ceased. In many parts of the country, non-Hindu minorities continue to live in an atmosphere of fear and intimidation.

On all counts then, the spell of a super-naturalistic, superstitious and irrational religiosity has only grown in recent years and shows no signs of abating in near future. And by all accounts, this kind of religiosity continues to serve as a breeding ground for religious nationalist sentiments.

It is this context that makes the central idea of the book relevant. To quote a key passage from the first edition:

> This book is a plea for a serious and critical engagement with…Hinduism. Unlike those who think that any critique of religious reason implies either elitism or atheism, I believe there is a third alternative, namely, keeping religion within the limits of reason, making religious cosmology answerable to scientific knowledge and scientific method. Religion as a source of spiritual solace – yes. But religion as a source of understanding the workings of the natural and social world – no.

This project of making religious conception of the world answerable to scientific reason is the key to secularization of our cultural commonsense. Without this kind of secularization and disenchantment, secular laws enshrined in our Constitution will always remain ineffective.

This edition reproduces the three original essays, with minor editorial corrections. It also includes a more recent essay titled 'How Modern Are We? Cultural Contradictions of India's Modernity'. Inclusion of this essay strengthens the arguments in the rest of the book, while updating the reader regarding the deepening of the spell of dharma.

It is my sincere hope that readers will enjoy this new and improved version of the book.

Introduction

Fascism, writes Robert Paxton, can appear wherever liberal democracy is sufficiently implanted to be accused of producing class/caste divisions and decline, but not implanted deeply enough to resolve these crises through democratic means.[1] In societies with weak liberal cultures, the gap between the promise and the reality of liberal democracy gets filled up with dreams of a mythic Golden Age of greatness and goodness. Unable and unwilling to lay down any serious challenge to the material and cultural causes of the social malaise, these societies can only set their compass by a mythic past, which they try to (re)create through advanced technologies made available by modern science.

With the rise of Hindu nationalism, Indian democracy has taken a fascistic turn. Hindutva parties are in the process of redefining the ideals of democracy, secularism and social justice into the idiom of Vedic Hinduism. The same Vedic and Vedantic ideas of dharma, karma, varna and reincarnation which have allowed the most insidious inequalities and irrationalities to plague India throughout its history, are being celebrated as the ultimate resources for India's revitalization. Vedanta, one of the most reason-defying and reality-denying traditions, is being re-described as the mother of modern science. The resurgence of the "Hindu mind" is being promoted as necessary for the regeneration of not just India, but the entire planet. India is being re-defined as a Hindu nation, with Muslims and Christians cast as the sources of Mother India's "defilement and degradation."[2]

The meteoric rise of the Hindutva movement, from a virtual pariah to the ruling party in barely a decade, exposes the shallow roots of secular culture in India. The Hindutva phenomenon is – and should be – a cause of deep concern to all who hold India's welfare close to heart. But its rapid rise should surprise no one.

The rise of Hindutva was a disaster waiting to happen. Hindutva is not a reaction to the "hyper-rationalism" of colonial-Orientalist Enlightenment, but a sign of its historic weakness in India. The rapid rise of Hindu nationalism is not a "natural" response to the excesses of state-imposed and Eurocentric notions of secularism, as has been claimed by neo-Gandhian indigenists like Ashis Nandy, T.N. Madan, Dipesh Chakrabarty and other self-described anti-secularists and postcolonial intellectuals. (Interestingly, the Hindutva intellectuals mirror their anti-secularist critics in claiming credit for rising up against the "colonization of the Hindu mind" by Western-style "pseudo-secularism".)

Evidence from the fifty-plus years of postcolonial India shows no pattern of state-enforced, top-down secularism being forced down the throats of reluctant masses. India is no Iran under the Shah, or even Turkey under Ataturk. Far from it. Hinduism has thrived as the de-facto religion of the Indian state, with relatively less or more openness, under the Nehru and the mother-and-son Gandhi regimes respectively. Those who blame the wishy-washy, neo-Hindu brand of secularism practiced by Congress regimes for begetting Hindutva, mistake the personal biases of Nehru and other stray secularists as actual state policy. In actual fact, secularism in

India, as interpreted by the courts and policy-makers, has allowed active state interference in and sponsorship of all religions. The pressures of electoral politics have ensured that under the cover of "equal respect," the functionaries of the state freely indulge in Hindu rituals and customs in public institutions. Hindutva is different from other well-known cases of religious fundamentalist movements in the following sense. In the United States, Christian fundamentalism arose as a defensive reaction against the hegemony of liberalism in mainstream Protestant churches and in the society at large. In Iran the Islamic revolution took place in response to forced modernization of the society. Hindutva, in contrast, is not a reaction to the excesses of Western-style secularism, but a beneficiary of the neo-Hindu indigenization of the concept of secularism as tolerance of all orthodoxies.[3]

Hinduism has never confronted the full force of a rational critique of its metaphysical foundations. Given the peculiar circumstances of its birth, cultural nationalism, rather than a self-critical Enlightenment, has been the defining spirit of independent, postcolonial India. The 19th century Renaissance quickly turned into a full-scale Hindu revival. Anti-colonial nationalist fervor saw to it that a rational critique of Hindu metaphysics, inspired by the introduction of modern scientific discourse by the British colonists and missionaries, quickly gave way to reinterpreting scientific reason itself into Hindu metaphysical terms. From Ram Mohan Roy to Vivekananda, Aurobindo to Radhakrishnan, and even to some extent Nehru himself – that is, all the leading lights of neo-Hinduism – the naturalism and skepticism of modern science was declared to be either already contained in the Vedic literature, or declared to be of secondary status as compared to the ultimate spiritual truths of Vedanta. The Indian bourgeoisie, allied with the culturally backward peasantry under the influence of Gandhi, has been the active promoter of scientization of Vedas and, conversely, Hinduisation of science. The only consistent and uncompromising voices for a rational examination and reformation of the core values of Hindu metaphysics and ethics came from Dalit and shudra intellectuals, including above all, Ambedkar, Phule and Periyar. The work of the Enlightenment that was shouldered by the bourgeoisie in the West, fell upon the most oppressed and powerless sections of the Indian proletariat. The Indian left, unfortunately, never engaged with the religious questions with the seriousness it reserved for the economic injustices. Apart from the stray secular-humanist voices of M.N. Roy here, and D.D. Kosambi there, the organized left in India did not take up the cause of Hindu Reformation and the Enlightenment.

Thus, there were no substantial pressures on the Indian public culture to be secularized, and Hinduism to become disenchanted and rationalized. While India declared itself to be a secular state, its public culture was anything but secular. While we claimed to live by secular and democratic laws, these laws meant nothing in our everyday lives, either in the private sphere of family, marriages, kinship and friendships, or in the public sphere of work and government. Every obscurantist practice under the sun – from astrology to spirit possession and faith-healing – has continued unchecked, often with the full blessing of the state, and with open participation of public officials elected to uphold secular laws.

Unfortunately, Indian intellectuals were not free from cultural nationalism either. Even though – or because? – they came into their own as intellectuals through their training in social and natural sciences which first flourished in the West, they have remained defensive about the indigenous traditions. Since the 1960s when the Western theory itself began to take an anti-Enlightenment/postmodern turn, Indian intellectuals have turned into full-fledged nativists. Their calls for "alternative science" and "alternative modernity" rooted in indigenous worldview and an Indian civilizational dynamic are not different in substance from similar calls for "Vedic sciences" and "authentic" modernity issuing from Hindutva nationalists.

Given the entrenched traditionalism of the Indian elite, politicians and intellectuals, made fashionable by postmodern trends in social theory, is it any surprise that the Hindutva virus has spread so fast and so widely across India? Societies with rampant religiosity are breeding grounds for religious fundamentalist movements. Popular religiosity does not, by itself, necessarily lead to religious conservatism or religious nationalism. But in those societies where traditional religiosity forms the common sense of the masses, religious nationalists have an easier time coming to power.[4] The popular support for the Ram temple, the religion-tinged enthusiasm for the nuclear bomb, the periodic irruption of murderous rage against Muslim and Christian Indians – all these are anchored in a worldview justified by traditional religiosity, preached by innumerable gurus, glorified in the mass media and even taught in schools. Faith is not innocent of the crimes committed under religious ideology, for without anchoring itself in the faith, religious ideology will not have the mobilizing power it has.

This book is a plea for a serious and critical engagement with Hinduism. Unlike those who think that any critique of religious reason implies either elitism or atheism, I believe there is a third alternative: keeping religion within the limits of reason, making religious cosmology answerable to scientific method and scientific knowledge. Religion as a source of spiritual solace – yes. But religion as a source of understanding the workings of natural and social world – no. This separation is all the more important for Hinduism because Hinduism is a monistic religion which draws no dividing lines between nature and the supernatural (Brahman or the World spirit), or between natural laws and moral laws. Dharma is conduct which is in accord with nature of the cosmos itself.

The essays in the book have been written in an ongoing debate with Western and Indian postmodern/postcolonial and feminist critics of science. I believe very strongly that the postmodern and social constructivist philosophies of science deny the universality and objectivity of modern science, legitimating all local knowledges to be at par with scientific knowledge. This kind of epistemological populism does not help those in the non-Western world it is meant to be in solidarity with. Non-Western cultures do not need the condescending declarations of "modernity of traditions" from the West. They need a substantive equality in knowledge so that they can liberate themselves from *all* oppressions, Western *and* home-made.

The essays in the book simultaneously defend the enterprise of modern science and call for deploying scientific knowledge as a cultural weapon against the Hindu understanding of the world. I take on the call of Ambedkar (see chapter 2) and plead with Indian intellectuals to complete the project of Indian Enlightenment that he started.

The other essays connect the dots between postmodernism and Hindutva. The thread that connects all three essays is my conviction that the only sure way to defeat Hindutva is to struggle for secularization of Hinduism. Only by realizing the unfulfilled potential of the Enlightenment in India can we hope to defeat the fascism that is staring us in the face.

Notes

1   Robert Paxton. 1998. The Five Stages of Fascism. *The Journal of Modern History*, Vol. 70 (1): 1–23.

2   David Frawley, a k a Vamadeva Shastri, describes India as "Divine Mother, defiled and degraded, both by the inertia of her own people and by foreign enemies who cannot appreciate her spiritual beauty." The solution? The awakening of the "Hindu mind" which will "spiritualize" Western science and "regenerate the whole planet". See Frawley (2001), *Hinduism and the Clash of Civilizations*. New Delhi: Voice of India. These sentiments are the regular fare of Hindu nationalist discourse. See N.S. Rajaram (1998), *A Hindu View of the World*. New Delhi: Voice of India.

3 For a fuller analysis of the weakness of secularism and Enlightenment in postcolonial India, see the second chapter of my book, *Prophets Facing Backward: Postmodern Critiques of Science and Hindu Nationalism in India* (Rutgers University Press and Permanent Black).

4 See Nikki Keddie, "The New Religious Politics: Where, When and Why do Fundamentalisms Appear?" *Comparative Study of Society and History*, 1998: 696–723. Keddie argues that high degree of popular religiosity is a necessary (though not a sufficient) cause of the rise of religious fundamentalist movements. Keddie's hypothesis states: "Significant new religious political movements tend to occur only where in recent decades, religions with supernatural and theistic content are believed in, or strongly identified with, by a large proportion of the population. In addition...a high percentage of the population identifies with the basic tenets of its religious tradition regarding god or gods, its scriptural texts and so forth. The only single word for this phenomenon is...religiosity."

Dharma and the Bomb
Postmodern Critiques of Science and the Rise of Reactionary Modernism in India[1]

Of Fireflies and War

Amidst the headlines about nuclear-war worries in South Asia, a little noticed news item appeared on the BBC World News on May 14, 2002.[2]

The BBC reported that in the middle of the dangerous military build-up along the border with Pakistan, with careless talk of nuclear war in the air, the Indian government started funding scientists in the nation's premier defense research institutes to develop techniques of biological and chemical warfare based upon Arthashastra, a 2,300 years old Sanskrit treatise on statecraft and warfare. The venerable old Sanskrit book is supposed to include recipes for "a single meal that will keep a soldier fighting for a month, methods for inducing madness in the enemy as well as advice on chemical and biological warfare," according to Shaikh Azizur Rahman, the BBC reporter from Mumbai. Space scientists and biologists are trying to replicate the ancient formulas for feeding the soldiers a ration of special herbs, milk and ghee (clarified butter) that will keep them going for a month without food. Other projects include "shoes made of camel skin smeared with a serum from owls and vultures that can help soldiers walk hundreds of miles without feeling tired…A powder made from fireflies and the eyes of wild boars that can endow night vision…a lethal smoke by burning snakes, insects and plant seeds…" Rahman reported that scientists next plan to turn their attention to other ancient manuscripts which "claim to provide secrets of manufacturing planes which cannot be destroyed by any external force and remain invisible to the enemy planes." The scientists are reported to be "excited about the possibilities and do not for a moment think that the idea is crazy."

What is one to make of it? Comic relief? Wishful thinking (if only all our weapons came out of fireflies and boars and insects and plants…)?

Looked in isolation, this is just a funny little story, a side show. After all, what does this minor project matter when India continues to spend millions of rupees (close to 18 percent of the national budget each year) for developing or acquiring modern methods of mass destruction?

But this is no side show. This project is not about defense. It is about Hindu supremacy. This project is not aimed at an external enemy, but at extending the reach of Hindu nationalism in the public sphere. This project is about the rising tide of reactionary modernism in India.

To place this incidence in a larger context, let us go back to May 1998 when India test-fired nuclear devices in the desert of Pokharan.

The Bomb: India Goes Nuclear

A few years ago, the media around the world carried a picture that should have sent a chill down our collective spines. It showed crowds of ordinary, everyday, men and women, dancing in the streets of New Delhi to celebrate India's successful nuclear tests. (Think about it: *celebrating* the making of a nuclear bomb.) For these mobs, the technological hardware of the bomb was a symbol of their national greatness, their strength and even their virility; it was a Hindu bomb against the Islamic bomb of Pakistan. It is not a coincidence that many among the jubilant mobs cheering India's technological prowess also serve as foot-soldiers in the Hindu nationalist crusade against all those who refuse to accept the equation of India with Hindu Dharma. Such persecuted minorities include not just Muslims and Christians, but also secular artists, writers, filmmakers and political activists accused of disrespecting Hinduism. An India that celebrates its bombs, is an increasingly intolerant and illiberal India.

Anti-nuclear activists and progressive intellectuals in and from India, struggling valiantly to retain some degree of hope for a return to sanity, have argued that these pictures pander to Orientalist expectations of India – ignorant, nationalist third-world know-nothings. The Western media's emphasis on mobs celebrating the nuclear tests, the critics claim, misrepresent the actual sentiments of the majority of Indian people, who by-and-large, are opposed to nuclear weapons, or are at least indifferent to them. The overwhelming public approval for the prospect of India building the bomb captured by public opinion polls, the argument goes, was a statistical aberration stemming from the bias of the poll-takers for urban folk with telephone connections.

For the sake of peace in the subcontinent, one can only hope that this optimistic reading of Indian public opinion turns out to be true. Yet, the fact remains that while the Hindu nationalist supporters came out in the streets, with the full backing and blessings of the ruling Hindu nationalist party, the silent majority remained, well, silent. The scattered, albeit impassioned, protests by Communists, feminists and other left peace and disarmament movements failed to bring out the presumably disapproving majority – if it is really disapproving – into the streets.

While it may be difficult to accurately gauge the width and the depth of nationalist sentiment in the Indian public, the jubilant mobs cannot be easily dismissed as a statistical aberration or as an Orientalist stereotype created by the Western media. These mobs are only the visible signs of a large ideological counter-revolution that has been going on behind the scenes in schools, universities, research institutions, temples and yes, even in supposedly "progressive" new social movements organizing to protect the environment or defend the cultural rights of traditional communities against the presumed onslaught of Western cultural imperialism.

Dharma: Hindu Packaging of the Bomb

I will have a lot more to say in the rest of the paper about the anti-modernist tendencies of the Gandhian, postmodernist and old economic nationalist, anti-imperialist left alliance. But for now, I want to focus on how the bomb and the science behind it are being packaged in a Hindu idiom and propagated in schools, temples and the entertainment media as an unfolding of a holistic, unified, ultra-modern science already contained in ancient texts of the Hindus.

The ideologues of Hindu nationalism and indeed, many Indian scientists and ordinary people on the streets, claimed that the bomb was foretold in their sacred book, the Bhagwat Gita, in which god declares himself to be " the radiance of a thousand suns, the splendor of the Mighty One...I have become Death, the destroyer of the worlds." If Robert Oppenheimer used the Hindu imagery after the first nuclear test in 1945 to express fear and awe at what science had wrought, the Hindu partisans see in this imagery a cultural and religious justification for their nuclear weapons. Indeed, some observers have gone so far as to claim that the detonation of the nuclear bomb was a *religious* phenomenon in which Indians saw "the triumph of divine power... the workings of providence, grace, revelation and a history guided by an inexorable faith".[3]

There is plenty of evidence for a distinctively Hindu packaging of the bomb. Even though the Hindu nationalist BJP government responsible for the blasts eschewed religious rhetoric in its official pronouncements, it gave its parent organization, the RSS (Rashtriya Swyamsevak Sangh) and its cultural arm, the VHP (Vishwa Hindu

Parishad) a free rein to claim the bomb for the glory of Hindu civilization and Vedic sciences. Shortly after the explosion, VHP ideologues inside and outside the government vowed to build a temple dedicated to Shakti (the goddess of energy) and Vigyan (science) at the site of the explosion. The temple was to celebrate the Vigyan of the Vedas which, supposedly, contain all the science of nuclear fission and all the know-how for making bombs and much much more. (It is this ancient science that the defense ministry wants to tap into, as the BBC story reveals). Plans were made to take the "consecrated soil" from the explosion site around the country for mass prayers and celebrations. Mercifully, the fear of spreading radioactivity scuttled these plans.

But the Hinduization of the bomb has continued in many other ways: there are reports that in festivals around the country, the idols of Ganesh were made with the atomic orbits in place of a halo around his elephant-head. These "atomic Ganeshas" apparently brought in good business. Other gods were cast as gun-totting soldiers. At an official level, the weapons and the missiles under construction are given distinctly mythological names from Agni (the fire god) to Trishul (trident, the symbol of god Shiva). The religious imagery was sufficiently pronounced to have alarmed a group of religious-studies scholars in America. They issued a letter of concern to "protest the use of religious imagery to glorify and to legitimate nuclear exercises."[4] Indeed, invocation of gods in the context of nuclear weapons has become a constant feature of public discourse. During the current stand-off between India and Pakistan, India's most popular newsmagazine, *India Today*, prefaced its tasteless warmongering with references to Mahabharata and the "thousand suns". The net result of these references is to turn these ugly developments into something like the Mahabharata, in which god sided with the virtuous.

The invocation of goddesses of shakti and vigyan is not fortuitous at all. Hindu nationalists have claimed that the bombs and the missiles are symbols of India's advanced science and technology, the roots of which lie in its ancient religious traditions. The idea of constructing a temple to goddess of learning at the site of the explosion was meant to propagate the age-old popular myth that Vedas presage all important discoveries of science, especially quantum and nuclear physics. A popular version of this myth was reported by Jonathan Parry in 1985:

> In Benaras, I have often been told – and I have heard variants of the same story elsewhere – that Max Muller stole chunks of the Sama-Veda from India, and it was by studying these that German scientists were able to develop the atom bomb. The ancient rishis (sages) not only knew about nuclear fission, but they also had supersonic airplanes and guided missiles.[5]

The sacralization of war has meant a simultaneous scientization of sacred Hindu texts. Technological modernization, even in its most ugly form, is being encompassed into the traditional, religiously sanctioned understanding of the natural world.

Of Satellites and Horoscopes

Exactly the same pattern unfolded in another episode, this time involving satellites and horoscopes.

In April 2001, the Indian Space Research Organization made history by successfully putting a satellite into the geo-stationary orbit, 36,000 km. above the earth. In July 2001, the University Grants Commission, the central body overseeing funding of higher education, announced its plans to offer courses in Vedic astrology as science courses in India's universities and colleges. Astrology has been declared to be at par with other natural sciences and will be offered as a part of natural science curricula. This is in addition to other new courses including training in *karmakanda* (priest craft), Vedic mathematics and other "spiritual sciences". Other courses in "mind sciences", including meditation, telepathy, rebirth, mind control are being planned. The same space power that takes justified pride in its ability to touch the stars, will soon start educating its youth in how to read our fortunes and misfortunes in the stars and how to propitiate the heavens through appropriate *karmakanda*. For all we know, the satellites launched by India's own launch vehicles might some day carry internet signals that will make horoscopes easier to match!

To outsiders, the ruling Hindu nationalist government likes to present a face of enlightened, forward-looking democracy. Since the September 11 disaster, India has presented itself to the West as an ally in its fight against Islamic fundamentalism. This image hides another reality. Under the cover of democracy, the terms of political discourse in India are changing. Nominally secular institutions in the public sphere – from education and research to the media and government agencies – are increasingly adopting an aggressively Hindu identity.

The Hindu justifications for nuclear weapons, the attempt to read modern science into Vedic texts and the teaching of Vedic astrology as a science – all of these have to be understood in the larger context of Hindu nationalism. When you put these symbolic gestures in the larger context of the BJP sponsored research into Vedic sciences, the Hindu nationalist project of rewriting the history of Indus valley civilization as the cradle of the "Aryan" civilization, the alteration of school text books to Hinduize the curricula and to actively seek religious legitimation for economic and social policies, the Dharma and the bomb connection does not seem as "Orientalist" as some may think.

A Symptom of Reactionary Modernism

I submit to you that this Hinduization of the bomb is a sign of a phenomenon best described as reactionary modernism in which a society embraces modern science and technology, while rejecting the ethos and the ethics of the Enlightenment, or to put it another way, where technological modernization occurs without the benefit of secularization and liberalism. This phenomenon was first named and described by Jeffrey Herf (1984) in his well-known book, *Reactionary Modernism: Technology, Culture and Politics in Weimar and the Third Reich.*

What makes Herf's study of German Fascism relevant for contemporary India is his thesis that the Nazi support for cutting-edge technology and sciences was not merely a strategic bow to modernity to further an essentially irrational and anti-modern agenda. Rather, Herf argues – as I will in the case of India – reactionary modernism in Germany was underpinned by a distinctive, philosophically sophisticated worldview which, to quote Herf: "incorporated modern science and technology into the cultural system of German nationalism, without diminishing the latter's romantic and anti-rational aspects." Rather than allow modern science and technology to challenge the romanticism and wholism of the volkish ideology, German reactionary intellectuals, including Ernest Junger, Carl Schmitt, Oswald Spengler and Martin Heidegger succeeded in selectively assimilating science into the language of community, nation, kultur and finally blood and race. Modern science was disarmed of its critical potential by turning it into an expression of the "Aryan soul" and rejecting whatever could not be so distorted to fit.

Three Theses

I am now in a position to state three theses that I will expand on as I move along.

One, under the jargon of cultural authenticity, Hindu nationalists are in the process of absorbing science into myth, making science simply a belated, Westernized and distorted affirmation of the truths already known to Vedantic metaphysics of non-dualism and wholism.

Two, the political legitimacy of, and the philosophical arguments for this reconciliation of science and myth have been prepared not by the Hindu right but by self-described "progressive" intellectuals and activists who broadly share the postmodern suspicion of modern science as a metanarrative of binary dualism, reductionism and consequently, domination of nature, women and Third World people. In India, for at least two decades now, it is the populist anti-capitalist left that has identified the Enlightenment and science as the biggest obstacles to creating a good society. The demand for an indigenous, "patriotic" science has been the loudest among the intellectuals and activists who identify themselves as progressive in politics but indigenist in their cultural beliefs. The left-postmodernists hoped that once non-Western peoples, especially women and other oppressed groups among them, are allowed to bring their own cultural values and life-experiences into knowledge production, they will heal modern sciences' divide between facts and values, reason and emotions, nature and culture. *The Hindu reactionary modernists have claimed these same wholist, non-logocentric ways of knowing not as a standpoint of the oppressed, but for the glory of the Hindu nation itself.* The Hindu right, in other words, enthusiastically accepts the left's diagnosis that objectivity and value-freedom of modern science is the source of alienation and domination, but then it offers the high-Brahmanical view of the world – the same world-view that has, incidentally, legitimized the caste system and a stifling form of patriarchy – as the ultimate source of a non-alienating, non-dualist science. Whereas the postmodernists were concerned to expose the presence of myth and metaphysics in objective science of nature, the religious right has turned the argument around, and declared myths to be science.

This brings me to my last and more positive thesis: traditional cultures contain in them rudiments of materialist, pragmatic thinking which, far from being incommensurable and different, is perfectly compatible with the worldview of and methodological demands of modern science. In India, these proto-sciences have existed not in the mystical idealism of the Vedas and the Upanishads, but in the heterodox non-Brahmanical traditions of Lokayata and

Carvaka. *These* aspects of traditional cultures, when updated through rigorous scientific education, can serve as seedbeds of a secular and liberal culture in non-Western societies. Thus contrary to the prevailing wisdom among feminists and multiculturalists, who look to idealized "local knowledges", as alternatives to *modern science,* I insist that modern science is the standpoint of the oppressed in the Third World.

In the rest of this paper, I am going to expand on these three points. But as you well know, this whole issue of nature of science and other ways of knowing has been at the heart of the so-called science wars. I know I am entering a minefield here. So I want to take a minute to clarify the terms of the debate.

The Terms of the Debate

First, I want to make it clear that I do *not* see all the good and honorable people who seek solutions to the dilemmas of modern life in traditional societies, religions or in some other kind of non-instrumental community life as reactionary revivalists or backward-looking romantics. I most emphatically do *not* condemn any and all attempts to retrieve a usable past from non-Western heritage as reactionary. (As you will see in the next chapter on Ambedkar, the Buddha and John Dewey, I myself look back into India's intellectual history in order to retrieve cultural roots of the Indian enlightenment from the heterodox anti-Vedic philosophies). What concerns me about the particular retrieval that has gone on under the postmodernist-Gandhian-ecofeminist alliance is that the Brahmanical past they are retrieving is usable only for a new authoritarian Hindu nationalism.

One has to grant that the indigenist-left critics of modernity have the best of intentions. If they have quarreled with the Enlightenment, it is because they seek to extend its promise of tolerance and autonomy to other cultures so that they are not forced to conform to one universal story. If they quarrel with science, it is because they think it has become a new source of mystification and domination. I also do not deny that, apart from some notable crossovers, the anti-Enlightenment left in India has taken a firm stand against Hindu nationalism. Indeed, far from being knowing allies of the right, the indigenist-left intellectuals and activists are facing persecution from the current regime. While I acknowledge their courage and good intentions, I do question the soundness of their diagnosis of the ills of the modern age and the efficacy of their prescriptions for "non-Western modernities". What worries me is that after all the years of denigrating any rational critique of indigenous cosmology and traditions as elitist, or Western or both, the left's present stand for secularism may be too little, too late and too rife with self contradictions.

Second, my critique does not apply to all of postmodernist tradition but only to the so-called science question. Postmodernism at its best aspires to be an equal opportunity nay-sayer: *if* it denies the possibility of truth beyond the local contingencies of language and power, it denies it as much for the holy truths of Hinduism, or Christianity or Islam as it does for the grand narrative of modern science. While some Third World adapters of postmodernism try valiantly to remain even-handed and take a skeptical, deconstructive look at the grand narratives of their own traditions, in most cases, they end up as essentialists when it comes to their own heritage, and deconstructivists when it comes to the West. But *all* non-Western postmodernists, religious or lay, left or right, *without exception*, resolutely decry one particular grand narrative – namely, modern science. The very rationality and aspiration of modern science and the Enlightenment project more broadly – namely, the ability to put the inherited givens of a culture, paradigm or a mode or life, to a systematic, collective test of reason and experience in order to arrive at knowledge that transcends the confines of the given – is considered theoretically impossible, and politically flawed. It is seen as a peculiarly Western propensity and a source of its colonialism and other pathologies. When I criticize postmodernist influences in postcolonial thought, it is this view of science that I am concerned with.

Thirdly, following the lead of neo-Gandhian anti-modernists like Ashis Nandy, Vandana Shiva and others, many have become convinced that the very logic of science must be questioned, because modern science-based development has led to an absolute and growing immiserization and cultural displacement of women, native peoples and traditional family farmers. They also claim that development has given the state a *carte blanche* to coerce people, to tinker with traditional community practices and such. Science, as the phrase goes, has become the reason of the state.

I will cite only two counters to this thesis. One, contrary to the critics' claims, the fact is that nearly all indices of human development have more than doubled in the last two and half decades in India. And I am talking here of the Amartya Sen-inspired Human Development indices of such things as life expectancy, literacy and gender equality complied by the United Nations Development Program, and not some econometric data from the World Bank or IMF. Yes, the rate of improvement is uneven with women and lower castes lagging behind. Yes, India could have done much better had it paid attention to the basic needs of those on the bottom, without sacrificing economic growth. But this is a far cry from saying that things have gotten worse or that people are getting poorer in absolute terms. Secondly, in one of the rare qualitative studies of this kind, the well-respected agronomist N.S. Jodha found some interesting results which challenge the conventional wisdom of modernization as a source of hardship and anomie. Jodha found that over a period of two decades, even those villagers in Western India who had not seen an increase in real incomes reported a significant increase in well-being. The villagers felt their lives were getting better because they did not have to depend upon the patronage of their caste superiors, they no longer felt compelled to follow inherited occupations for they had more choices and greater access to modern amenities. Freedom from patronage, opportunities for individual choices, a belief in progress: all these are modern liberal aspirations which these villagers had discovered for themselves. Many of these improvements, incidentally, were made possible thanks to the state intervention, the same state that is treated by postmodernist critics as authoritarian and colonial in its mindset.

What I am trying to get to is this: the despair over the violence of modernity is totally disproportionate to the facts on the ground. While much remains to be done, the situation does not call for a total condemnation of modernization.

Hinduization of Science

Qualifications and clarifications out of the way, let me now return to the three theses I laid out.

Let us start with Hinduization of science. I mentioned how the bomb is being packaged in the idiom of dharma, complete with atomic gods. The Hinduization goes much deeper. *All* of modern science is in the process of being knitted into a new Indo-centric, Aryan science. If I may borrow a term from Louis Dumont, what we are witnessing is a process through which high Brahmanic Hinduism is encompassing modern science into itself. That is to say, Hinduism is presenting itself as already containing the worldview, the methods and even the findings of modern science, especially of quantum physics, ecology and medicine. Science simply becomes a somewhat inferior, materialistic aspect of Vedic wisdom. (Encompassment is the traditional Hindu way of dealing with heterodox ideas. It leaves room for different views to be accepted at their own terms, but always tends to include them in a hierarchic relation subordinated to the ultimate truth of dharma. The other is not recognized in its otherness against which one's own beliefs can be tested, but claimed as an aspect of, approach to, or aberration from the truth contained in its own doctrine.)

This notion of Hinduism-as-science is a part of the nationalist myth which recurs repeatedly in the writings of 19th and 20th century reformers including Ram Mohan Roy, Vivekananda, Dayanand, Gandhi and to some extent, even Nehru. These reformers hoped to revitalize and modernize Indian culture not by a reformation and an Enlightenment-style critique of traditional ways of thinking, but by a *restoration* of the supposedly scientific spirit of the ancients.

With the Hindu nationalists in ascendance, this idea of Hindu dharma as science has moved, once again, to center-stage. The government is funding research projects to modernize astrology, Vastu Shastra, Vedic mathematics, Vedic physics and traditional medicine. New books have appeared, some of them co-authored by US-based scientists in important universities and sold aggressively around the world through Amazon.com. These books claim to have found such modern discoveries as electricity and microscopes, the solar spectrum and cosmic radiation, photosynthesis and plastic surgery, binary numbers and advanced computing techniques in the Vedas. Specifically, these scientists claim that the number of syllables in Vedic verses, which supposedly corresponds to the number of bricks in fire altars and the number of beads on the rosary, actually encodes the exact distance between the moon and the sun, the speed of light, the Big Bang etc. With the Hindu nationalists at the helm, these discoveries are quickly finding their way into school text books.

This is not all. Claims for Hinduism-as-science are part of the larger argument that equates ancient Hindus with the original Aryan speaking people. In the emerging Indo-centrism, the land mass of India is claimed to be the original home of the Aryans who presumably took the Vedic myths and concepts to ancient Egypt and Greece. Thus, the Indo-centrists claim, Egyptian and Greek sciences, and by lineage, modern science, are Hinduism's "daughter sciences", or at least "sister sciences". Hindu India becomes the cradle of all civilization.

This self-aggrandizing Indo-centrism would be laughable if it were not so dangerous. It is laughable because it makes preposterous claims based on shoddy logic and even shoddier evidence. It is dangerous because these claims are made with an earnest nationalistic fervor, backed by the state which is committed to making India Hindu. There is a need to be concerned with Hinduism-as-science not so much because of the harm it can do to the growth of modern science and technology, but because of the harm it can do to the development of a secular and egalitarian public culture in India. Hindu ideologues are not going to close down the labs: they are hitching their prospects for entry into the club of elite nations on nuclear, computer and genetic technologies. Hinduism-as-science is a part of the cultural project of modernizing without allowing the rationalism and secularism of the Enlightenment to challenge the traditional cultural values. Declaring – by definition – Hinduism as the mother of all science, gives gloss and prestige of modernity to rituals and institutions which are based on a magical understanding of the natural world and a hierarchical understanding of the social world.

Such a glossing is not without serious political consequences. It is true that ideas do not drive history. But the choice between invoking the authority of ancient texts and transcendent myths or seeking publicly testable evidence makes a huge difference to the quality of debate and the terms of sociability in the public sphere. This need for creating new democratic norms of sociability is nowhere greater than in India which has one of the most liberal Constitutions, superimposed on a society that lives by the idea of natural inequality. The danger of Hindu science is that it will further entrench the holistic, organismic worldview as our national ethos, and a source of public morality. Moreover, absorbing science into myth and rituals – the hallmark of reactionary modernism – makes the defense of religion appear like a defense of reason and modernity, and brings out the mobs in the streets who want to become modern without losing their traditional identities.

Postmodernism as an Ideology of Reactionary Modernism

So far so good. But recall that I am making a bigger and – to some – more controversial claim; i.e. that the postmodern and postcolonial denigration of modern science has provided the philosophical grounds for Hindu science. On the face of it, my thesis sounds highly implausible. Whereas the Hindu right is busy claiming the products of modern science and technology as a part of its own heritage, the postmodernist and postcolonial intellectuals have sought to *insulate* non-Western cultures from modern science, which they see as alien and oppressive. When the postmodern critics turn to local cultures and "ethno-sciences", they are not seeking to establish these as the mother of modern science. On the contrary, the whole point of ethnoscience has been to establish that non-Western cultures can produce *wholly different sciences* informed by pacific, cooperative, womanly values of nurturance and sustainability which would never lead to such things as nuclear bombs. How can I ignore all these differences and impute the postmodernists of aiding and abetting the project of Hindu science?

As I said at the outset, it is not the intentions but the *logic* of postmodernist critics of science that has opened the door to the religious right. A logic which denies distinctions between myth and science, ideology and knowledge, might and right runs the risk that myth, ideology and might will be clothed as scientific truth. And that is what has indeed come to pass in India today. But more specifically, there are at least three postmodernist arguments against science which one finds repeated, almost verbatim, in the arguments for Hinduism-as-science. These are: one, arguments against dualism as a source of domination of the other; two, arguments for critical traditionalism and standpoint epistemology; and three, arguments for epistemic charity. In order to understand why these arguments would have a resonance for Hindu nationalists, it is important to understand how they argue their case.

The case for Hinduism as science hinges on Hinduism's purported wholism or non-dualism which does not differentiate between the domains of the material world and the spiritual and social world: all aspects of the entire cosmos are supposed to be products of pure consciousness and eventually merge back into it. Conveniently forgetting that this unity is a purely metaphysical and mystical unity, not accessible to the ordinary human sensory experience or reason, the Hindu nationalists elevate it to the level of a science – the Hindu equivalent of the unified field theory! – that grasps the interconnections of the world. They correspondingly elevate yoga and other traditional methods of divining associations between heavens and earth as legitimate Hindu methods of science which are supposed to be as rational within the unified cosmopolis of Hinduism as the experimental method is within the Judeo-Christian dualism between a transcendent law-giving God and his creation.

This holism would have remained a fantastical romance, but for the tremendous philosophical support it has found from the postcolonial, feminists and ecofeminist critics of science. Critiques of dualism and binary thinking lie at the heart of these critiques of science as a source of domination. Let me explain.

Gayatri Spivak, a self-described "deconstructivist, feminist Marxist", defined her role as a postcolonial critic as someone who can say an "impossible no" to Western conceptual categories which she as an intellectual inhabits most intimately. Why did she and many other bright, erudite diasporic scholars from India feel compelled to renounce western concepts, which as Spivak admitted, are an intimate part of their intellectual heritage? They, like the rest of the "new humanities" in North American universities, have taken a linguistic turn: they have come to see Western knowledge itself as a source of colonial power, for it was by objectifying, quantifying and classifying the colonized, that the Western powers had been able to control it. Colonialism ceased to be political-economic domination, but came to be seen as an epistemological domination, a *colonization of the mind* by alien conceptions of what is real, what is right and what is desirable. While it was possible for earlier critics of imperialism to oppose the economic and political domination of the West but still accept the universality and legitimacy of Western science, postcolonial and other influential anti-Enlightenment intellectuals demanded that a critique of imperialism must mean decolonization of the mind and culture. The only true progressives were those segments of Indian population – the peasants, the traditional masses – who lived their lives in community and harmony, as fish in the water, unselfconscious of the bases of these traditions and unsullied by the rationalism and materialism of modern science and Enlightenment. This position was first developed by neo-Gandhian intellectuals led by Ashis Nandy and others at the Center for Study of Developing Societies and the scholars-activists associated with the Patriotic and People's Science and Technology group, who drew upon Kuhn, Feyerabend and the 60s critics of instrumental reason. They were later joined by feminist and postcolonial critics who are influenced by feminist standpoint epistemologies and Foucaultian equation of knowledge and power.

I submit that this demand for decolonization of mind is nothing but a demand for a holist or re-enchanted science which leads straight to Hinduism-as-science. The heart of postmodern, feminist and postcolonial critique has been that modern science is dualist, that it differentiates and separates the domains of culture from nature, knower from the known, matter from spirit, reason from myths and emotions, public from private etc. But the postmodernists claim, reason is preferred over emotions, objectivity over an open embrace of cultural values, not because they bring us closer to truth, but because they further patriarchal and imperialist goals. This dualism is the source of "epistemic violence" because it forces the "other" to conform to the categories that serve the ends of power. It has became axiomatic in feminist and science studies that women and non-Western people appreciate interconnections, they don't think in binaries but in wholes. This was the whole point of critical traditionalism of neo-Gandhians like Ashis Nandy, ecofeminists like Vandana Shiva. This position had strong sympathies with feminist standpoint epistemologies, which also saw women as less prone to dualist thinking. Any doubts regarding the validity of feminist or non-Western knowledge are put aside by using sociology of science arguments—which I call epistemic charity—which claim to have shown that all claims to truth are equally socially constructed and none can claim to bring us closer to truth.

India was a fertile ground for these ideas, *not* because India is suffering from a real bad case of mental and economic colonialism – as the critics of modernity claim – but because of the populist, anti-modernist orientation of Indian intellectuals, a legacy of Gandhi's conservative revolution. Indeed, neo-Gandhians including such influential figures as Ashis Nandy, Vandana Shiva, Claude Alvares, Ziauddin Sardar were the major conduits between science studies, postcolonial studies in the West and the popular movements at home. These are important public intellectuals, with a substantial following in new social movements. In my book, *Prophets Facing Backward: Postmodern Critiques of Science and Hindu Nationalism in India*, I document how these ideas spread through the ecofeminist and people's science movements in India. In practical terms these ideas have meant a defense of the moral economy of the peasant including the gender and caste relations of traditional family farmers and their caste-based local courts, an opposition to urban industrial intervention in rural affairs, an organized opposition to development projects, sometimes overriding what the local people themselves wanted, a staunch anti-Americanism which translates into ridiculing liberalism and human rights, but above all, an overwhelming desire to learn from, respect and cherish "the people". Any critique of the people's self-destructive customs and objectively false knowledge is frowned upon as elitist and rationalist. Indeed, "rationalist" has become one of the worst insults that can be hurled at an intellectual. Interestingly, these exercises in postmodernism-inspired populism fed-back into science studies and feminism as evidence of the standpoint epistemologies and alternative sciences.

If these good populists ever take the time to read the right-wing critiques of modernity, they will have to, if they are honest, admit a shock of recognition. The populist defense of moral economy of traditional India is nothing other than the philosophy of "Integral Humanism" that is the official doctrine of the ruling Hindu nationalist party. As I mentioned above, the epistemological harmony and non-dualism between nature and culture, between individual and collective, between facts and values that ecofeminists and feminist standpoint epistemologists celebrate is precisely what Hindu science celebrates as Vedic epistemology. The cooperation, nurturance and harmony the Gandhian and postmodernist proponents of marginal knowledges celebrate is precisely what the integral humanists celebrate as the Hindu idea of a good society in which different castes are bound to each other as limbs to a body. The critical traditionalism of Ashis Nandy and the postcolonial insistence upon recovering the indigenous conceptual framework is precisely what the nationalists demand when they insist that Hindu Dharma should guide what we take from the West.

These resonances are not lost on reactionary modernists and they have actively sought to co-opt the indigenist left's initiatives in order to win respectability. Indeed, leading ecofeminist – Vandana Shiva – has become a leading light of Hindu ecology and makes regular appearances in neo-Hindu ashrams in north America. Her work is most respectfully cited in *The Organiser*, the official journal of RSS, the cultural arm of Hindu nationalist parties. India's leading feminist, who long ago took the culturalist turn and formally joined Ashis Nandy's group, is routinely interviewed and cited in neo-Hindu publications. The work of ethno-science scholars Dharampal and Claude Alvares, is cited with great admiration in Hindu science texts. What is more, the populist left opposition to the Green Revolution, genetically modified crops and other science intensive initiatives, is routinely co-opted by the ultra nationalist, autarkic elements of the Hindu right, as are their more constructive programs for reviving traditional technologies.

The tragedy is that in the rush to denounce dualism of modern science, the critics have completely overlooked one essential fact: the lack of separation between nature and culture, matter and spirit of the much ballyhooed wholism of Indian ways of knowing has traditionally provided the cosmological justification for India's peculiar institution, namely caste. The natural inequalities of human beings and their separation into hierarchical though intimately interconnected castes is not an aberration of Hinduism but justified by the central dogmas of dharma and karma. These dogmas depend upon a unified understanding of nature and culture: the distinctions between human beings are justified by distinctions in the very order of nature. Indeed, the real victims of oppression – namely, the untouchables and other lower castes – understood the hoax of dualism very well. It was for this reason that they have been the staunchest supporters of the Enlightenment in India. The interests of the oppressed are served by breaking the cosmopolis and demanding, unlike the Hindu science, that our knowledge be equally accessible to all through sensory experience and reason.

In conclusion, what I have described is a wedding in progress: a wedding of science with myth, superstition and nationalism. Such a wedding was not ordained by circumstances, but was arranged by well-meaning but ultimately dangerous philosophers. This is one marriage I am afraid is going to last until a whole lot of violence and hatred and misery finally do the two apart. For the sake of all that is decent, I hope against hope that this union ends in a speedy divorce.

Notes

1   This is the text of a paper I read at the annual convention of the American Sociological Association, July 2000 held in Washington D.C.

2   "Indian Defense Looks to Ancient Text" by Sheikh Jazzier Raman, BBC News, May 14, 2002 at http://www. bbc.co.uk/

3   Harman, William, Speaking About Hinduism and Speaking Against It. *Journal of the American Academy of Religion*, Vol. 68, No. 4: 733–740.

4   The text of the letter can be found on the website http://www.acusd.edu/ theo/risa-l/archive/msg00782.html.

5   Parry, Jonathan. The Brahmanical Tradition and the Technology of the Intellect. In Joanna Overing (ed.), *Reason and Morality*. London: Tavistock Publications. p.206.

A 'Broken' People Defend Science
Reconstructing the Deweyan Buddha of India's Dalits[1]

Intellectuals have a choice to make, Max Weber wrote in his well-known essay, "Science as a Vocation". They can either act as political partisans or as teachers, but they cannot claim to be both without doing irreparable harm to the entire society. As partisans of political positions, ("demagogues," Weber calls them) intellectuals are free to deploy their words and their ideas as "weapons…as swords against enemies", in order to canvass for their side. But as teachers and scholars, it is incumbent upon them to treat ideas not as swords, but "as plowshares to loosen the soil of contemplative thought" (Webcr 1922: 145). Idcas can only be used as plowshares, Weber insists, if we cultivate the temperament of a scientist toward them, that is, treat ideas dispassionately and without fear or prejudice of their political implications.

In recent years, Weber's distinction between swords and plowshares and between teachers and demagogues has been actively contested. Weber's shield against demagogy – a dispassionate, scientific stance toward ideas – has been declared to be a myth and a farce. Social constructivist critics of science, along with their feminist and postcolonial allies, have not only discoursed about science with a passion that belongs more appropriately to a war, they have tended to reduce the worldview, the methods and the content of modern science to a sword that the powerful wield against the powerless. Modern science understood both as a body of knowledge and as a way of knowing, has come to be seen as a construct and an enforcer of Eurocentric and patriarchal norms. The interests of the oppressed, it is claimed, will be better served by developing "alternative epistemologies" grounded in their own standpoints and their own cultural values. While local knowledges of non-Western peoples and/or women are given the "epistemic privilege" to challenge modern science's claims to objectivity and universality, the latter is denied all relevance for bringing about a reasoned change in worldviews and ethical values in non-Western societies.

For example, Sandra Harding, a leading feminist epistemologist, has recently claimed that it is merely a sign of "civilizational Eurocentrism" on the part of the West to pretend that modern science is rational, objective and universal. In reality, the very methods and content of science are "deeply and completely… co-constructed" by the modern West's Eurocentrism and patriarchy (Harding 1998: 54). What is more, Harding claims that the vulnerable groups in non-Western world actually experience the purported value-freedom and objectivity of science as a "rude and brutal cultural intrusion", because they "do not value [value]-neutrality; they value their own Confucian, or indigenous American, or Islamic or Maori…or Judaic or Christian values", (1998: 61). Helen Longino has argued that feminists must join postcolonial peoples, especially the more oppressed among them, to develop an "oppositional stance" toward the dominant ideology coded into the "background assumptions, language, models and arguments and theories" of modern science (Longino 1997:117). Well-known postcolonial critic, Ashis Nandy echoes this sentiment, arguing, "there must be skepticism against science [because] modern science is the basic model of domination of our times and is the ultimate justification for all institutionalized violence" (Nandy 1988: 121–122). Indeed, repudiation of modern science as an advance over other ways of knowing has become the first principle of post-colonial and post-development studies (Nanda, 2001). For these "new cynics", to borrow Susan Haack's (1993a) apt epithet, modern science has ceased to be a source of organized skepticism against dogma, but has become a new dogma that requires a radically skeptical scrutiny from the standpoint of its "victims".

What is truly amazing about this neo-cynical agenda is that it fails to even acknowledge – let alone allow any substantive role in understanding the place of science in society – this simple but inconvenient historical fact: namely, there are many instances in the non-Western world, when those who suffered the worst indignities and injustices heaped on them by "their own" cultural-religious values, were the first to *embrace* modern science, connect it to their traditions of inquiry, and claim it as their own. One such example comes from India, where the victims of India's hierarchical caste order – the untouchables, or dalits (literally, the "broken" or "crushed" people)[2] – have been among the most ardent advocates of a de-sacralized (i.e., naturalistic) and scientific understanding of the natural world. Far from experiencing the objectivity and value-freedom of science as a "rude and brutal intrusion," important dalit-feminist intellectuals have *celebrated* the contents and the methods of modern science as a source of demystification of the Brahmanical Hindu understanding of nature as permeated with Brahman, the divine spirit. Since Hinduism justifies untouchability and caste hierarchy as being in accordance with the order of nature itself, the content and the method of modern science have obvious attractions for the victims of caste prejudices.

In this chapter, I hope to bring to light a remarkable confluence between dalits' aspirations for freedom, and the naturalist tradition best represented in the classical pragmatists' call for subjecting all inherited worldviews and values to the test of scientific method. I will examine how the leading dalit intellectual of the 20th century, Bhim Rao Ambedkar (1891–1956), a man revered as a liberator by millions of his admirers, appropriated John Dewey's view of 'scientific temper' for challenging Hindu metaphysics and cosmology, and the ethics of natural inequality they sanction. Ambedkar studied at Columbia University (1913–1916) and was deeply influenced by Dewey, at that time a professor of philosophy at Columbia, and the nation's best-known public intellectual. Ambedkar attended Dewey's lectures, read his books and took his ideas home with him. Back in India, after many years of civil disobedience against caste discrimination, and after a long, frustrating fight against Mahatma Gandhi's paternalistic reformism, Ambedkar, along with nearly a million of his fellow untouchables, publicly renounced Hinduism and converted to Buddhism.

I believe that how dalits understand science and why they find it empowering hold important lessons for the contemporary critics who see science as an obstacle to empowerment. Ambedkar followed Dewey in finding in modern science an attitude, a temperament, that had the potential to challenge unexamined tradition and prejudices by cultivating a collective, democratic "will to inquire, to examine, to discriminate, to draw conclusions only on the basis of evidence after taking pains to gather all available evidence…to treat all ideas as working hypotheses to be tested by consequences they produce" (Dewey 1955[1938]: 31). What is more, Ambedkar followed Dewey in believing that the *content* of modern scientific theories demanded rational acceptance by *all* people, universally, because these theories are the products of the most systematic practice of the scientific attitude. He believed that with modern science, a new kind of knowledge was born that could replace the theological, metaphysical and supernatural foundations of knowledge accessible only to the pure and the wise, with the fallible, testable experience of reality available to all. Ambedkar, again like Dewey, believed that the most important task facing intellectuals was to reconstruct the inherited cultural values and social ethics by bringing the spirit and the content of science to bear upon them: science had metaphysical and ethical implications, over and above its instrumental uses. Ambedkar would have actively resisted the critics, who in the name of liberation and empowerment, seek "new" norms of science in the pre-scientific, metaphysical and often supernatural worldviews to challenge the working assumptions of modern science. The whole project of "alternative sciences" would have seemed to him more like turning the clock back on the hard-won progress modern science has made in learning how to learn.

As I will try to show in this paper, Ambedkar carried his commitment to a Deweyan scientific temper into his understanding of the Buddha. I will offer a reading of Ambedkar's *Buddha and His Dhamma*, the bible of neo-Buddhists, to show that Ambedkar understood the Buddha as a Deweyan pragmatist and a scientific critic of the status quo. Ambedkar turned Dewey's call for reconstructing philosophy and society in the light of scientific inquiry into the central message of the life of the Buddha–with good justification, for the Buddha (563–483 BCE), after all, was a rebel against the mystical idealism of Brahmin priests in his own time. I will argue that Dewey's ideas helped Ambedkar make the historic rebellion of Siddharth Gautama relevant for his own quest for a civic religion of 'equality, liberty and fraternity' in India. Dewey was by no means Ambedkar's only inspiration: powerful 19th century anti-caste movements in his own province were important influences, as were the histories of numerous heterodox, anti-Vedic, materialist sects/schools that have always existed on the fringes of Hinduism. But I contend that Dewey, and his American experience more generally, served Ambedkar as a bridge between the past dalit traditions of protest, and a self-consciously liberal and secular worldview. By emphasizing scientific temper as the central message of the Buddha, Ambedkar made respect for systematic inquiry a part of religious obligations of dalit neo-Buddhists.

While Dewey's influence on the Chinese Enlightenment, the May 4th Movement is very well documented (Westbrook, 1991), as is his continuing influence in China today (Youzhong 1999), his indirect connection with the aborted *Indian* Enlightenment is hardly known outside the small circle of dalit scholars and other students of Indian social movements. Unfortunately, even these scholars tend to treat Ambedkar's American experience and his great regard for Dewey as just one more biographical detail, 'counting for very little' (Zelliot 1992: 85).[3] There is very little appreciation of either the formative influence Dewey's philosophical ideas had on Ambedkar's thinking, or of their possible relevance for the contemporary struggles for secularism and democracy in India. Even more problematic is the relativist talk of 'a different voice' for dalits that is making its appearance in some segments of dalit community, albeit not without strong protest from others.[4]

This paper is a contribution toward recovering the Dewey-Ambedkar-Buddha connection. The chief aim is not so much to add to the rich intellectual history of American pragmatism, although that would be a wonderful bonus. The motivation is to retrieve the ideas of Dewey – the original Dewey as Ambedkar understood him, and not the 'hypothetical' postmodernist Dewey made popular by Richard Rorty[5] – in order to dispel the cultural despair that has befallen Indian intellectuals and their allies in Western academia. I hope to ride the rising tide of pragmatism in North America and Europe to bring back a Deweyan respect for scientific temper to the continuing *Kulturkampf* in India against elements of Brahmanical Hindu cosmology that proclaim permanent inequalities to be built into the very nature of some categories of people, natural objects, foods, occupations and even gods themselves. Even more importantly, I hope to bring out the relevance of Ambedkar–Dewey synthesis for the creation of a secular and humanist civic culture which can, hopefully, combat the rising religious nationalism in India today.

I will fill in the details of the Ambedkar-Dewey synthesis of scientific temper through an engagement with the feminist and postcolonial critics of science who argue for 'alternative sciences' based upon the values that the experience of marginality presumably confers upon women and other offshore underdogs. This may, at first glance, appear to be a rather tortuous way to recover Ambedkar, for surely this dalit Dewey can be understood in his own terms. Yet, a juxtaposition is necessary to highlight the uniqueness of Ambedkar's quest and to recover its radical potential in today's intellectual climate. Feminist and postcolonial critics have emerged as the leading theorists of 'emancipation'. Their understanding of the very rationality of modern science as inimical to a good society has come to dominate the imagination of academics and activists to such an extent that any defense of modern science as potentially emancipatory gets labeled as a throwback to 'positivism' or 'Orientalism'. For the Ambedkar–Dewey synthesis to reclaim its understanding of modern science as a force for demystification and democratic inquiry, it has no choice but to dispute the terms of the debate set by the contemporary theorists of 'alternative' and 'emancipatory' science(s).

The first two sections will juxtapose the feminist and postcolonial view of experience and cognitive values with how Dewey understands them. The third section will describe Ambedkar's struggle against the Hindu legitimation of caste, and his eventual conversion to Buddhism. The fourth section will delineate three main teachings of Ambedkar's Buddha which sanctify inquiry carried out in a spirit conducive to modern science as a source of enlightenment and freedom: *prajna* or creative intelligence, 'religion of principles' against a 'religion of rules' and finally, the 'associated life' of civil society that is bound by, and defers to, *prajna*. The concluding section will examine the social and philosophical significance of Ambedkar's Deweyan Buddhism.

1. Feminist Epistemology, or the Importance of Being an Underdog

> *One of the tenets of feminist research is the valorization of subjective experience.* Helen Longino (1990: 190).

Helen Longino is correct. "Valorization of subjective experience" is indeed the raison d'être of feminist epistemology. But it is *also* its Achillies heel. How can valorizing the subjective experiences of the oppressed avoid valorizing – if not actually revitalizing – those worldviews and values that allowed the oppression to go on in the first place?

It will be my goal in this section to show that the cluster of "interactionist values" derived from women's lived experiences has profoundly conservative implications for non-Western cultures. Celebration of the underdog values, as Hilary Putnam has argued (1992:185), "immunize(s) the rationales of oppressions in other cultures from criticism". Invocation of non-Western values of non-dualism, nature-culture holism and ecological consciousness may provide a vantage point to criticize modern "Western" science, but it has nothing whatsoever to do with "emancipation". On the contrary, Ambedkar and other dalit-feminists have been struggling *against* the non-dualist holist knowledge that feminist epistemologists and neo-Hindu apologists celebrate. Modern science was important to Ambedkar (as to Dewey) precisely because it could *break* the continuity between the natural and the social order, so that the latter could be questioned and changed.

This immunization of traditions follows from a fundamental asymmetry between facts and values that lies at the heart of feminist epistemology: *while all statements of facts about nature are seen as value-laden, social and cultural values themselves are conceptualized as cultural givens, and beyond the pale of rational criticism and reasoned change.* This asymmetry explains the radical challenge feminist and other identity-based epistemologies pose to the spirit of the Enlightenment. The project of the Enlightenment is premised on the assumption that new facts about the world and new methods of justification of beliefs will help revise inherited values and make them more conducive to human autonomy and equality. The fundamental task of philosophy, as Dewey never tired of emphasizing, was "evaluation of values" in the light of modern science. Feminist epistemology renounces this task.

The asymmetry between facts and values is not a regrettable oversight. Rather, it follows from the central dogma of post-Kuhnian "Strong Programme" of sociology of scientific knowledge, namely, that true beliefs in science are as much caused by the interpretation of data through our socially-embedded and race-, class- and gender-differentiated metaphors and values, as are false beliefs (Bloor 1991). Thus, Sandra Harding has insisted, our most well-confirmed sciences – our "best beliefs" – are no more exempt from race, class and gender relations than the social beliefs and behaviors of "health profiteers, the Ku Klux Klan or rapists" (Harding 1991:12). Because scientists bring the dominant values of a society into the laboratory, scientific facts encode these values, despite the provisions for transformative criticism that have become institutionalized through the evolution of modern science (Longino 1990, Harding, 1991).[6] Surreptitiously carried into "facts" dominant social values can only affirm and legitimize, but can never challenge, social values, either inside the lab or in the society at large. Not better-warranted facts, but only more politically progressive values imported from outside the mainstream can challenge the mainstream values. Thus Sandra Harding's case for "strong objectivity" and Helen Longino's insistence upon "doing science as a feminist". In plain language, "the technical is political" (Hess 1997a: 160) or "science is politics by other means", (Harding 1991: 10) and requires political solutions for advancement.

As a corollary, the Strong Programme sociologists extend a stance of what I have previously described as "epistemic charity" (Nanda, 1998) toward pre-modern, non-Western knowledge systems. They allow no epistemologically significant distinctions to be made between the findings of modern science and any other knowledge system: all institutionalized beliefs about nature are equally contingent upon social interests and cultural meaning (Barnes and Bloor 1982).[7] In such a world, it becomes conceivable that other societies, differing only in their social values, would arrive at different and incompatible beliefs about the same domain, and that all would be equally rational, because evidence itself is relative to the social values. To take an example, Harding argues (1998: 20) that it is not the case that Newton's law of gravity will cease being a valid law, but alternative sciences will produce alternative explanations of gravity, which will be equally valid and equally universal and which need not necessarily converge, in the long run, with Newton's laws. In plain language, all sciences are "ethno-sciences", modern science being the ethno-science of the West (Harding 1998).

Having accepted the social constructivist dogma, feminists and postcolonial critics face a dilemma. If all knowledge systems are cultural constructs, so are women's sciences, and non-Western sciences. How, then, to argue for a *feminist* epistemology, especially in a postcolonial flavor?

The solution to this dilemma is the well-known feminist standpoint epistemology, a feminist version of the Biblical promise that the meek shall inherit the earth. "Women of color", having suffered devaluation and oppression under the joint assault of andocentrism and Eurocentrism, now joined together in an "oppositional consciousness" to Enlightenment humanism, will develop a "successor science" that will make it possible for women to become knowers without compromising their womanliness (see especially Harding 1986, 1991 and Haraway 1991).[8]

These underdog successor sciences will be marked by all those characteristics that the conventional sciences presumably lack—receptivity to complexity and an attitude of holism, non-differentiation or non-dualism that does not separate parts from the complex whole, nor separate mind from the matter, or the subjective (emotions, values) from the objective description of nature. Despite challenges from postmodernist feminists who question *all* claims of "better" accounts of reality (Hekman 1997), interactionism continues to be recognized as a hallmark of feminist knowledge which gives it authority as a better and/or less distorted *science* rather than just another perspective.[9] Interactionism as a feminist virtue claims that sciences done from a feminist standpoint – that is, a standpoint that treats women's social experiences under patriarchy as relevant to warranting scientific facts – will find dynamic, interactive, non-dualist relationships between elements of nature, rather than the reductionist, and hierarchical, "master-molecule" models of control presented as "facts" by science-as-we-know it. The meek shall put together what the powerful have torn apart.

But why should the underdogs see the whole in its totality and dynamism? The argument for interactionism are familiar. Because material life structures consciousness, women's subordinate role in the sexual division of labor – as mothers, daughters and wives – has epistemological consequences. Women's "relationally defined existence", results in a "world-view to which dichotomies are foreign" (Harstock 1999: 120). Consequently, women as subjects do not separate themselves from the objects under their care. Their relationship with the world is necessarily less differentiated, more relational, more acutely sensuous than the merely instrumental interchange men have with nature. Rather than demand women to fit into the masculine ideal of objectivity, women should legitimately use their relational approach to the world as a cognitive resource.

Interactionism opens the door to Third Worldism. The standard argument is that women from traditional, non-Western societies, are more "epistemologically privileged" than their Western sisters, for their bonds with family and nature haven't yet been severed by modernity. Third World women are the original postmodernists, the first cyborgs: unlike Western/Westernized scientists who abstract and objectify nature, they experience forces of nature as a continuum with their own everyday experiences in producing and sustaining life. Abstraction is male, oppressive and *Western*, while interaction is female, liberatory and *Eastern*.[10]

Even those feminist epistemologists like Helen Longino who are weary of privileging any special female experience, biological, social or both, end up endorsing the interactionist agenda on purely political grounds. If all science is inescapably shaped by background assumptions of a culture, Longino has argued, then feminists should feel perfectly justified in bringing in values that are "consistent with the values and commitments [they] express in the rest of [their] lives" (1990: 191), without having to argue that these values reflect a special female experience. In her more recent work, Longino (1995, 1996, 1997) has refined this choosing-to-do-science-as-a-feminist argument by drawing up a list of six "feminist virtues" (accuracy, novelty, ontological heterogeneity, mutuality of interaction, applicability to human needs and diffusion of power). These virtues are meant to operationalize the feminist interactionism as found in the work of Harding, Keller, Haraway, postcolonial ecofeminists and others. Longino urges feminist scientists to use these values, instead of the standard Kuhnian values for theory choice,[11] to interpret the evidence from scientific experiments. Because all epistemic values carry political valence, and Kuhn's values apparently have conservative political implications (Longino 1996:54, 55), feminists must use feminist cognitive values so that they can "reveal gender" in nature, science and culture.

Longino argues, for example, that feminists need not aim for the time-honored value of simplicity which aims to explain a maximum of observations with a minimum of entities and laws. Treating simplicity as a truth-enhancing value reflects reductionist, conservative and generally masculine political attitudes, Longino claims, because it reduces the entities and phenomenon being explained to mere epiphenomena of more fundamental ("privileged") laws. Because *women as social beings* have found their individual subjectivities subsumed under masculine traits parading as universals, *women as feminist scientists* should refuse to seek simple theories in the domain of nature as well. They must instead actively look for complex interaction between distinct particulars which cannot, by definition, be explained by any other more fundamental entity.

Even more startling is Longino's advice to feminist scientists to actively seek out novel theories and models that "depart from accepted ones", purposefully "disregarding consistency with other theories" (1997:124, also 1995, 1996). Her argument is that it is legitimate for feminists to jettison the traditional value of consistency of new findings with what we already know because "mainstream traditional frameworks have been used in accounts that neglect female contributions …or treat as natural alleged male superiority" (1997:122). In other words, because existing science is a patriarchal construct, feminists need not worry if their scientific claims contradict the existing body of knowledge in any field. As long as feminist theories can adequately explain the experimental data, interpreted through the background assumption provided by feminist virtues, they are no less justified than theories justified by gender neutral, universal values that Kuhn and others favor.

This invitation to disregard external consistency with the existing body of knowledge lethally weakens Longino's earlier emphasis on shared public standards as a constraint on subjectivism in science. If feminists, and *mutatis mutandis*, any other community of scientists, are free to construct scientific theories by postulating "different entities, processes, different principles of explanation, alternative metaphors" (1997:122) which are chosen *because* they contradict the existing stock of knowledge and the existing background assumptions, how can there be *any* shared, publicly recognized standards at all that can be used to evaluate the claims of these sub-communities? If feminists disregard the coherence and reasoned acceptance of their models and theories by the rest of the scientific community, are they not opting out of the process of "transformative criticism" that was meant to keep subjective biases under check? With the gradual loosening of the constraints of accepted standards,[12] feminist epistemology has in fact become an argument for alternatives *to* science, and not for alternative science in a feminist vein.

Longino's invitation to local communities to adopt cognitive standards that "express their aspirations" (1996: 55) runs the risk of opening the door to the worst excesses of Third Worldism and pseudo-science. Consider the following:

- David Hess (1997a: 49–51), an anthropologist of science, has interpreted Longino's call for novelty to argue that spiritism in Brazil need not concern itself with how it contradicts existing science. Longino's "feminist virtues" enable Hess to wrap up magical thinking in a progressive cover.
- Anthropologists like Fredrieque Marglin have used arguments very similar to Longino's to argue that the Indian folk belief in the goddess Shitala as a cause and a cure of smallpox is an example of "non-logocentric" science which does not separate nature from the culture's beliefs in the supernatural (Marglin 1990).
- Others like Ashis Nandy and Shiv Visvanathan (1990) have deployed the non-dualist values to defend the occult medical practices of theosophists like Helena Blavatsky and Annie Besant

as examples of "ethnoscience at its most autonomous". These supposedly "feminist" occultists were staunch supporters of the most conservative factions of early 20th century Hindu nationalists and were intellectual allies of the Nazis. [13]

• Indeed, Hindu nationalists themselves justify teaching Vedic astrology as a science in Indian universities and colleges by arguing that from within Hindu non-dualism of nature and super-nature, astral influences are part of nature and therefore a legitimate subject of scientific study (Nanda, 2001a).

• Similar examples can be multiplied many times from Harding's latest work on multicultural science and from the writings of ecofeminists who have raised back-breaking labor of peasant women into a resource of interactionist values for a new feminist science (Shiva 1986).

Such is the reach of these ideas that even some dalit and 'backward'-caste intellectuals and their allies have begun to romanticize the special, holist knowledge traditions. Some dalit and backward-caste intellectuals have taken an anti-modernist view and romanticized the knowledge-traditions of dalits. Scholars sympathetic to ecofeminism (Datar 1999) and Gandhian traditionalism (Nigam 2000) have argued that dalits should treat the disembedding from traditional communities caused by modern technology and capitalism, and not traditions themselves, as their primary cause of concern. These critics accept the postcolonial argument that modern secular worldview is silencing the experiential knowledge of dalits and women.

But these identitarian tendencies are kept in check by those who grant a very limited epistemological privilege to the raw experience of oppression. They admit that dalits "talk differently", but only in so far as their experiences give them access to problems that may not register as problematic to non-dalits. As Sharmila Rege (1998) has argued, given the preponderance of urban, upper-class/caste intellectuals in India's social movements, the concerns specific to dalits – the everyday indignities, violence and social apartheid – often get subsumed under the standard rhetoric about the working-class, the sisterhood, the environment etc. It is this silence that dalit intellectuals are trying to break. But by and large, dalit scholars show a salutary weariness with identiy-based epistemologies, for they fear that, "to privilege knowledge-claims on the basis of direct experience, on claims of authenticity, may lead to a narrow identity politics" (Rege 1998: WS44). They have raised questions if "experiential knowledge of dalits adds up to a 'knowledge system'? [Can it provide] tests of verifiability and validation?" (Guru and Geetha 2000: 133). To the extent these dalit modernists do privilege dalit culture, they privilege the proto-scientific aspects of it which are rooted in manipulation and control of nature in the process of production, which was the province of the laboring castes (Ilaiah, 1998).

The problem with the above scenario goes beyond epistemic relativism. The problem lies in immunizing non-dualist, holist values from a critique by glorifying them as a resource for better science. Feminist valorization of non-differentiated connected knowing suffers from a most grievous misunderstanding. It is simply not the case that holist ways of knowing are always and everywhere progressive or emancipatory. On the contrary, modern liberties – feminism included – became possible in the West only with a *separation* of the natural and the moral orders (Berger 1967, Gellner, 1988).

This misunderstanding has had the most disastrous significance for new social movements in India, because *holism lies at the very heart of caste and gender hierarchy in India.* The essence of holism is a lack of separation between subject (mind, consciousness) and the object (nature). Hindu holism introduces a supernatural element: nature and human societies are embodiments (or illusions, in the Advaita tradition) of the absolute spirit, Brahman. This imposes the claims of the natural *and* the sacred order on human subjectivity, ethics and morality: transgressions against the social codes simultaneously become transgressions against the natural and sacred order. Nowhere is the naturalization (and sacralization) of social order more evident than in the institution of caste. The caste hierarchies – with Brahmins (priests) at the top, the shudras (servants) at the bottom, and untouchables as beneath even the servants – are supposed to mirror the order of nature. Whether one is born a female or a male, a dalit or a Brahmin, is not an accident at all, but the working out of the natural laws of karma and rebirth that regulate the embodiment of Spirit. Castes, genders, animals, plants and inanimate objects are simply different forms of the same spirit, arranged in a chain of being, depending upon their karma or moral deeds. In this non-dualistic, inter-connected world, objects of nature take on moral significance (e.g., diseases are goddesses, animals and plants are auspicious for human life and purposes) while human morals have consequences for the natural order (e.g. women's sins can bring about death of her husband).

It is this conception of natural order – holist and interconnected to the very core – that Ambedkar was rebelling against. He turned to the "reductionist", "masculine" and "violent" sciences of the West for help. It was through his *guru*, John Dewy, that he learnt the significance of modern science for a revision of social values.

2. Dewey: Science and Revaluation of Values

> *The central problem of philosophy is the relation that exists between the beliefs about the nature of things due to natural science to beliefs about values.* John Dewey, *The Quest for Certainty*.

John Dewey, like the feminist and postmodern critics, sought a new unity in facts and values. But unlike the feminist and postmodernists, he did not treat values simply as cultural givens, beyond the reach of scientific facts or scientific method. His non-dualism worked both ways: facts act back upon values. Reconstruction of values in light of progress already made in natural sciences was the whole purpose of his naturalistic non-dualism. For Dewey, the metaphysical, non-verifiable holisms of traditional knowledge systems would not be resources for better science, but rather hypotheses for empirical inquiry.

Here I will highlight only those aspects of Dewey's philosophy that are relevant to the feminist critique of, and Ambedkar's defense of, modern science. I will refer mostly to Dewey's later works, especially *The Quest for Certainty* or QC (1929), and *Experience and Nature* or E&N (1925).

First, Dewey fully shared (indeed, anticipated) the feminist antipathy to a positivist conception of experience as a passive mirror of nature, and saw the "knowledge-experience" as always in interaction with the non-cognitive, affect- , habit- and tradition-laden spheres of social life. Yet, he would have seen the subjective experience of the underdogs neither as *prima facie* "privileged", nor an indictment of the existing corpus of scientific knowledge. Rather than take the experience of the subaltern – or of any particular group – as a vantage point for creating new rules of inquiry, Dewey called for extending the hypothetical stance of science to *all* "primary experiences" of all social groups alike, so that they are transmuted into "secondary experiences", that are "purified" and "enriched" by a process of systematic doubt and "regulated, reflective inquiry" by a democratic community of inquirers (EN). Experience born of oppression was not an indication of better insight, but a cry for help for education and enrichment.

Secondly, the hope that with the advancement of science, more and more of our accepted beliefs will be also be the most warranted animates the entire corpus of Dewey's writings. Rather than allow traditional authority of church, family and society to dictate what we will believe, beliefs tested through a collective and democratic process will gain the allegiance of all groups in an open society. Dewey insists upon and welcomes "a certain purification of traditional beliefs" by making them face the tribunal of scientific method (1950[1930]: 30, also QC). Dewey saw in the success of modern science concrete evidence that human beings are capable of creating their own regulative standards by subjecting their experiences to a collective, democratically conducted inquiry.

Finally, the "purification" of social values works by the same experimental logic of evaluation that Dewey proposed for scientific inquiry. On a Deweyan understanding of science, we bring values we learn from our varied experiences in all aspects of our lives into construction of scientific facts, but *our values themselves can be, and must be, warranted as any other judgment of fact.* Or as Hilary and Anna Putnam (1990: 410) put it, "any valuing can be evaluated", using the same method of inquiry that has amply demonstrated its success in natural sciences. Values, on Dewey's account, are not given to us by gods, neither are they social conventions and nor epiphenomena of material life. Rather values are ideas that guide conduct. In that capacity, they are means to solving a problem. They can therefore be rationally assessed in terms of their success or failure in solving the problem adequately. Thus, it should be an empirical question whether or not the values women, non-Western people and others derive from their experience of marginalization do indeed make for more reliable means of conducting scientific inquiry. Mere fact of oppression, or the goal of subverting male power cannot, a priori, validate the values and ends that follow from oppression or feminism.

The problem with post-Kuhnian philosophers of science is that they have relativized the success and progress in science that Dewey, Peirce and other classical pragmatists took for granted. Facts, epistemic values and goals of inquiry have all been rendered internal to a paradigm or a culture. But important developments in philosophy of science, especially by Susan Haack, notably her *Evidence and Inquiry* (1993) and also Haack (1998), and Larry Laudan, notably his *Science and Values* (1983), and also Laudan

(1996), have shown how the original pragmatist view of mutual self-correction between facts and values can still be defended, notwithstanding the Kuhnian revolution. Haack's influential crossword puzzle analogy provides a convincing argument for revaluation of values, as does Laudan's reticulational analysis. According to Haack, our background assumptions – our guesses, worldviews and biases, derived from habit, cultural traditions, or explicit political commitments – must face and adjust to the already completed entries in the crossword, just as the latter must remain open to revision in the light of the new clues our background assumptions lead us to discover. Laudan likewise argues for a mutual adjustment and justification of facts, values and goals so that we can use "our factual beliefs to drastically shape our views about what methods are viable" and "we can use our knowledge of available methods of inquiry as a tool for assessing the viability of proposed cognitive aims" (Laudan, 1983, p. 63).

The classical pragmatists and some of their contemporary interpreters show a way of employing the hard-won advances in factual knowledge and hard-won advances in learning how to learn, as resources for reconstructing other ways of knowing. These advances ought to make us weary of accepting at face value separate and unique cognitive goals of "feminist science" and/or "postcolonial science", especially when they allow the infusion of metaphysical, organic non-dualisms of traditional religions into scientific work. It was this progressive, naturalistic and anti-metaphysical view of science that Ambedkar imbibed from Dewey and read into the Buddha.

3. Ambedkar's 'Music in the Storm'

> *You took on the world*
> *You played with fire*
> *You played us music in the storm.*
> from 'Ambedkar: 1978. Equality for All, or Death for India', by Namdeo Dhasal.[14]

October 14, 1956 holds a special significance for the dalit community in India. On that day, Bhim Rao Ambedkar, by all accounts the most influential dalit intellectual of the 20th century, publicly renounced Hinduism and converted to Buddhism. He was not alone in this 'rebirth' as he himself described it:[15] close to half a million of his caste members accompanied him that day in taking the vows to stop praying to Hindu gods and to abide by the Buddha's teachings.[16] Ambedkar died shortly afterwards. He is reported to have spent his last hours on this earth putting finishing touches to *Buddha and His Dhamma*, published posthumously, translated into Marathi and Hindi, and accepted as a sacred book by neo-Buddhists in India.

Ambedkar's turn to Buddhism came at the end of a long quest for a faith that would allow him to anchor his spirituality in a worldview that did not denigrate his community's humanity. Turning to a reconstructed Buddhism was for him a necessary step toward destroying the metaphysical and cosmological gloss the core values of Hinduism put on hierarchy and natural inequality. His American experience and his Deweyan scientific temper, along with the anti-caste struggle of other low-caste rebels who had gone before him, all led him to the Buddha.

The biographical details are well documented.[17] Ambedkar was born in the lowly Mahar caste in the Western state of Maharashtra in 1891. Mahars were general-purpose village servants whose caste-duties included cutting wood for cremation, removing dead cattle, washing wells, delivering messages over long distances, among other things. The touch of a Mahar was considered polluting, and they lived in segregated areas.

As the British did not observe caste, they had no hesitation in making use of caste divisions to serve their own interests.[18] In the process, they unintentionally opened up avenues of education and employment (e.g. soldiers, cooks, waiters etc.) which used to be closed to the lower castes. Given the general-purpose nature of their caste duties, the Mahars were accustomed to trying out new occupations. As a result, a large number of Mahars enlisted in the British army.

Ambedkar was born in one such family. The army connection secured him an education in English, even though in segregated settings, complete with all the indignities reserved for his caste. He showed promise as a student. With financial help from an enlightened local royal, he was able to go to college first in Bombay, and later in the USA at Columbia University and England at the London School of Economics.

Ambedkar spent three years (1913–1916) at Columbia University, where he worked for his Ph.D. in economics. He seems to have availed himself of courses offered by 'as many top ranking professors at Columbia as he could, whatever their field', including Dewey, Edwin Seligman, James Harvey Robinson and Alexander Goldenweiser who gave him a 'broad and deep exposure to an optimistic, expansive and pragmatic body of knowledge' (Zelliot 1992). But it seems that Dewey was the closest to a *guru* Ambedkar had: he not only followed his ideas all his life but, according to his wife, Savita Ambedkar, 'happily imitated John Dewey's distinctive class room mannerism – thirty years after he sat in his classes'. (Zelliot 1996: 84). (Columbia University acknowledged the contributions of its worthy alumnus and conferred an honorary doctorate on him in 1952. Last year, the university installed a bust of Ambedkar on campus). It is not known, however, if Dewey was aware of the influence he had on Ambedkar, and through him, on the lives of millions of distant strangers. As far as I have been able to ascertain, the two were not in any direct communication, although there is some evidence that Dewey took sporadic interest in the anti-colonial struggles in India. After his Columbia years, Ambedkar went on to obtain a D.Sc. from the London School of Economics and to pass the bar exam, returning to India for good in 1923.

For more than a decade after this return, Ambedkar remained optimistic that political and economic changes – access to education, right to vote etc. – would suffice to integrate the lower castes into the national mainstream. Ambedkar, in other words, did not start out with the religious question. Like most other left-leaning social reformers of his day, he gave primacy to structural reform, expecting the religious and the cultural realms to fall in place. But the bitter struggles of untouchables to exercise their right to drink water from segregated village wells (the famous civil disobedience at Mahad), their right to enter Hindu temples hitherto closed to them (temple-entry movements of Pune and Nasik)[19] and his bruising debate with Mahatma Gandhi over the question of separate voting rights for outcastes (the famous Poona Pact of 1932 in which Gandhi prevailed) all led him to a realization that advancement of the untouchables was impossible without a prior reform of the core values of Hinduism. His disillusionment with Hinduism, and with largely upper-caste nationalism of Congress party which put political emancipation from the British above any urgency for internal social reform was complete by 1935 when he first declared his intent to renounce Hinduism. ' I was born a Hindu, but I will not die a Hindu,' he is reported to have told Mahatma Gandhi. Whereas at the time of Mahad civil disobedience in 1927 (where he famously burnt the *Manusmriti*, a sacred Hindu law-book that prescribes draconian punishments for breaking caste rules), Ambedkar believed that by uniting all Hindus in one caste the untouchables were 'rendering the greatest service to the Indian national and the Hindu community,' by 1935, he was urging conversion to secure freedom from the Hindu community: 'Our aim is to gain freedom. To reform the Hindu society is neither our aim nor our field of action' (Ahir 1997: 4,19). With this disillusionment, his quest for a new faith that can anchor his values of 'liberty, equality and fraternity' began in earnest. Given his deeply religious temperament, Ambedkar could not bring himself to turn his back on religion, the course taken by the non-Brahmin, self-respect movement of Periyar in south India, and recommended by most Marxists. Ambedkar's quest ended, twenty years later, with his conversion to Buddhism.

What does this religious conversion have to do with questions regarding the place of science and scientific temper in social life – questions that we are interested in exploring in this paper? The short answer is *everything*, because Ambedkar's Buddha was reason and scientific method sacralized. In order to appreciate the centrality of reason and naturalism in Ambedkar's reconstruction of the Buddha, it is important to understand the philosophical source of his disillusionment with Hinduism.

In his short and bitterly angry book, *Annihilation of Caste* (1936), Ambedkar asks why upper caste Hindus tend to treat their fellow beings with aversion, refusing participation in the 'associated activities' in everyday life–eating together, living together, working together, praying together, marrying into each other's families? His answer: they shun social intercourse with fellow human beings not because they are 'inhuman or wrong-headed…but because they are deeply religious' (p. 111). The myriad hierarchies and taboos of caste have the 'sanctity of the *shastras* [Hindu scriptures]… people will not change their conduct unless they have ceased to believe in the sanctity of the shastras' (p. 112). The real enemy, Ambedkar declares, 'is not the people who observe caste, but the *shastras* that teach them this religion of caste' (p. 111).

Ambedkar launches a bitter attack on Gandhi's reformist attempts to just say no to untouchablity, while publicly praising the divinely sanctioned *chaturvarna* (the four basic varnas or castes) as a source of harmony and community, an antidote to the West's individualism.[20] Ambedkar argues that untouchablity is not an aberration of Hinduism that can be rooted out by good works, moral exhortations or new legal codes. Rather, *untouchablity is a logical corollary of Brahmanical Hinduism's peculiar understanding of nature and its laws*, namely the law of karma. For Hinduism, karma is a theory of cause and effect that transfers causation from the realm of consciousness/spirit to the realm of nature/matter and vice versa: thus immoral karma in this and/or past lives ('karmic crimes'[21]) activate different proportions of five elements of nature ('*gunas*') in each person that make him/her innately more or less pure. Ambedkar arrives at this understanding of hierarchy as built into Hinduism's central dogmas through an exhaustive study of Hindu philosophical ideas, both as they appear in the sacred texts and as they circulate at the popular level.[22]

Given how Hinduism naturalizes and, at the same time, sacralizes inequality, Ambedkar argues, removal of untouchablity will require a 'notional change... a change in the state of mind' (p. 111). But the law of karma occupies the same explanatory status in Hindu epistemology as a bona fide law of nature. Because the famously non-dualistic Hindu ontology does not separate matter or physical nature from spirit or the moral realm, actions in the moral realm are admitted as eliciting equal reactions in the physical realm. Thus, assorted 'karmic crimes' can bring about anything from birth as an untouchable, to natural disasters as earthquakes, floods, droughts, disease etc. This peculiar nature of Hindu metaphysics, which rationalizes injustices and misfortunes as the natural consequence of the workings of laws of nature, led Ambedkar to an appreciation of scientifically justified laws of nature which can challenge the Hindu ontology.

There are two aspects of Ambedkar's call for annihilation of caste that are of great relevance to our engagement with the contemporary critics of science. One, in a complete refutation of those who condemn science and the Enlightenment as Eurocentric and colonial, Ambedkar was making a classic case for an Enlightenment-style critique of religious reason in India. He expressly and repeatedly invoked the ideals of the French Revolution – 'Liberty, Equality and Fraternity' – as the suitable ideals for democratic movements in India. What is more, like the *philosophes* of the French enlightenment, Ambedkar strove to give primacy to scientific reason as the new standard for a 'constant revision and revolution of old values' (Ambedkar 1936: 132). Far from non-Western culture valuing their own values over the value-freedom of science, as Harding claims, Ambedkar is unequivocal in his preference for the truth-enhancing values and methods of modern science of Galileo, Newton and Darwin, which he thought were fully commensurable with the teachings of the Buddha and the ancient non-Vedic materialists and skeptics.

In this he was not alone. Two other contemporary anti-caste movements – one led by Jotirao Phule, a 'touchable' but of backward caste, in Maharashtra, and the 'self-respect' movement, led by E.V. Ramasami (Periyar), in the Southern state of Tamil Nadu – had already emerged as a nucleus for an alternative form of nationalism which, unlike Congress, demanded not just freedom from the British, but also freedom from internal, homegrown oppressions. This is not the place to expand upon the historic connections between Ambedkar and these anti-caste movements.[23] What is relevant to us is the fact that modern science was understood by *all* these movements alike, not as just one among the many equally plausible ways to construct 'facts' about 'nature', but as a method that was an *advance* over the traditional Hindu epistemology, which assigned explanatory power to supernatural entities and forces that are in-principle unverifiable by human senses and reason. Indeed, Phule's high regard for natural philosophy and its use by radicals like Thomas Paine to challenge Christianity is well documented (O'Hanlon 1985),[24] as is Periyar's radical empiricism (Geetha and Rajadurai 1998). A *disenchantment* of nature, *breaking* the continuity of the divine spirit and the material, *separating* the real facts of nature from the dominant religious/cultural values were the urgent goals of these movements of the oppressed – all contrary to de-differentiation and wholism that the contemporary critics of science rate so highly in the name of the oppressed.

Secondly, at no point in his writings Ambedkar romanticized the experience of his fellow Mahars or any other oppressed caste, gender or tribe as a source of superior knowledge. His entire project was motivated by a great empathy and love for his long-suffering community, but this love never turned into a romance. The 'monster of caste' crosses *everyone*'s path alike, every which way you may turn: 'you cannot have political reform, you cannot have economic reform, unless you kill the monster [of caste]' (Ambedkar 1936: 5). Unlike some who claim that dalits' experience of oppression has made them egalitarian and non-patriarchal, entirely free from all Hindu legitimation of hierarchy (see Deliege 1999 for a review), Ambedkar recognized that the experience of oppression has also left them deformed and in need of repair: 'tolerance of insults and tyranny... has killed the sense of retort and revolt. Vigor and ambition have completely vanished from you. All of you have become helpless, unenergetic and pale. Everywhere there is an atmosphere of defeatism and pessimism...' (Ahir 1997:17). While he acknowledged that centuries of caste oppression gives the untouchable community a greater objective interest, than any other community, in annihilating rather than modernizing caste, he never forgot that untouchables had *also* internalized the Hindu world-view that naturalizes hierarchy, that they *also* recognized the distinctions of caste.[25] Indeed, that was one of the reasons why he felt that socialism in India was not possible without a prior rationalization of social consciousness of the working classes (Ambedkar 1936: 74), a position which put him at odds with both the Marxists and Gandhians.

On Ambedkar's account, the group interest of dalits in emancipation from social hierarchy gives them a greater urgency and a greater motive than any other social group in India to appropriate science, to learn its methods and its content and to give it a liberatory meaning by bringing it to question the ontological claims of Hinduism. Dalit interests, in other words, lead them not into a quixotic search for their own science that affirms their experiences and their values, but toward giving new emancipatory meanings of the sciences we have.

To summarize this section, Ambedkar answered the classic question facing all revolutionaries 'What is to be done?' with a bold call for annihilation of the worldview that allows and justifies caste. To accomplish this task he constructed a Deweyan Buddha.

4. Ambedkar's Deweyan Buddha

> *Be your own guide*
> *Take refuge in reason*
> *Take refuge in truth.*
> The Buddha's last words, as interpreted by Ambedkar.

Ambedkar's Buddha teaches how to bridge the gap between facts and values, between how we know about the world we live in, and how we treat our fellow beings. In a statement that recurs throughout his speeches, interviews, and writings, Ambedkar presents the Buddha as teaching *prajna* (understanding, as against superstition and naturalism, as against supernaturalism) in order to create bonds of *karuna* (empathy) and *samata* (equality). Of the three, *prajna* is central for without it, the other two can falter. Thus Ambedkar's Buddha teaches that 'the path of all passion and all virtue…must be subject to test of *prajna* or intelligence… because without intelligence, generosity may end up demoralizing and love may end up supporting evil' (Ambedkar 1957: 30). In more distinctively Deweyan terms, Ambedkar saw the Buddha as a prophet of a scientific ethos which, if given a chance to take root, can help create a civic culture that respects the fundamental values of 'liberty, equality and fraternity'.

It is how Ambedkar understands *prajna* and the centrality he assigns to it for democratic change where Dewey's presence

is most palpable, is where Ambedkar stands in stark contrast
to all contemporary advocates of 'alternative epistemologies'. In
Annihilation of Caste (henceforth *Annihilation*), written some
20 years before his magnum opus, *Buddha and his Dhamma*
(henceforth *Dhamma*) he had already explicitly evoked 'Prof.
John Dewey, who was my teacher and to whom I owe so much', to
define his project of fostering 'notional change' through reflective
thought.

Briefly, in *Annihilation* he urges his fellow Indians to forego the
quest for certain and absolute knowledge of the ultimate Truth of
Being, the kind of knowledge idealized by Brahmanical Hinduism.
In words that distinctly echo Dewey's (see footnote 5), he proposes
a new ideal of knowledge which embraces change, and which will
learn to constantly revise all that is taken as settled. His argument
is worth quoting in full:

> the Hindus must consider whether time has not come for them to
> recognize that there is nothing fixed, nothing eternal, nothing *sanatan*
> [sanskrit for eternal]; that everything is changing, that change is the law
> of life for individuals as well as for society. In a changing society, there
> must be a constant revolution of old values and the Hindus must realize
> that *if there must be standards to measure the acts and men, there must
> also be a readiness to revise those standards* [italics added](p. 132).

Ambedkar bases his call for transvaluation of values on two long
quotations from Dewey (without citing the source) to the effect
that it is our duty '*not* to conserve and transmit the whole of our
past achievements, but only as much as makes for a better future
society' (p. 131) and that we should not make 'the past a rival of
the present, and the present a more or less imitation of the past'
(131–132). The contrast with underdog epistemologies is clear:
inherited values are to be critically examined, not 'privileged' as
sources of better truths.

What will break the spell of the *sanatan* or the eternal is
reflective thought, which Ambedkar understands in a classic
Deweyan manner. Most of our life is unreflective and habitual, he

says. Only a situation that presents a dilemma forces us to reconsider our habits and the philosophical assumptions that support those habits (p. 121). He cites caste Hindus travelling in railway trains where it is impossible to maintain the customary caste distinctions as an example of such a dilemma. There are two ways, Ambedkar says, to deal with this crisis that modernity has engendered. One way is to follow what the Brahmanical scriptures commend, that is, to consult first the Vedas (the revealed knowledge), then the smritis (the law books) and only then *sadachar* (customary morality). This traditional 'solution' only legitimates a schizophrenic life in which 'a Hindu' accepts the modern technological conveniences like train travel, but then comes home and undergoes a *prayaschit*, or repentance, for breaking caste prohibitions. Following traditional values in a modern world will force 'a Hindu... to break caste at one step and to observe it at the next, without raising any questions' (p. 121).

Ambedkar is highly prescient here. Keeping the modern world of science limited only to technological gadgetry, but isolated from the values that guide the inner life and social ethics is now recognized as the major mechanism for the remarkable survival and continuity of traditional values in India (Singer 1972 and Roland 1988). Although most Indians (at least in urban areas) no longer come home and do penance for breaking caste rules, compartmentalization of things scientific for the outside life of work, and traditional virtues (including caste and all the cultural baggage they carry) for the domestic life of marriages, friendships, life-cycle rituals remains widespread. Indeed, traditional 'virtues' are thriving with the aid of modern technology: information technology has made caste-based marriages easier to arrange, and horoscopes more 'exact' and easier to match. (Postmodern and postcolonial intellectuals who celebrate the survival of the traditional in the civil society, obviously don't wish to perpetuate caste prejudices. But they tend to hold the continued existence and growth of such traditional virtues a lesser evil than the breakdown of community caused by forces of modernity.)

Ambedkar's preferred solution to this compartmentalization of scientific knowledge and social values bears the stamp of Deweyan thinking. His solution calls for breaking down the compartments between the instrumental and ethical implications of science. Ambedkar argues for actively using the same scientific revolution that replaced the bullock-cart with a train to reshape the Indian society's understanding of natural laws and its preferred modes of fixing beliefs. He argues for the need to develop new principles of validating facts, and then using these principles to judge if the traditional facts about the natural and social order are warranted (p. 123–124). He accomplishes this in his interrogation in *Dhamma* of the traditional Hindu cosmology that treats karma – the sum total of good and bad deeds that guides the immortal soul in its various rebirths – as a law of nature.

Before we look more closely at *Dhamma*, it may be useful to get a feel for this book. As mentioned before, this book serves as a holy book for Ambedkarite Buddhists, especially the more educated, urban Buddhists, and is used by them to solemnize marriages and births etc. The book is written in the style of the Bible, with parables from the life and teachings of the Buddha, interwoven with Ambedkar's own interpretations. The parts where Ambedkar tells the story of Siddharth Gautama's renunciation and his Enlightenment are truly moving, and allow the humanity and earnestness of the Buddha as a young man to shine through. There are, however, parts where Ambedkar turns didactic and tries too obviously to put his own 20th century spin on caste upon the Buddha. On these occasions, he is too rationalistic to satisfy theologians or even lay believers. In fact, some traditional Buddhists object to Ambedkarite Buddhism as blasphemy since it rejects the ideas of karma and rebirth, both of which are accepted by mainstream Buddhists. But one could argue that Ambedkar has applied the Buddha's injunction

– to treat nothing as infallible and eternal – to the Buddha's own teachings and reinterpreted them for the contemporary world. But in making the Buddha's historic rebellion against Brahmanical Hinduism contemporaneous, Ambedkar has remained faithful to the letter and the spirit of the original texts. The Buddhist scholar who translated Ambedkar's *Dhamma* from English into Hindi ascertained that, except for the part about the Great Renunciation, it is based upon classic Pali texts. The 464 references Ambedkar makes to Buddhist texts come from the Pali *Tripitaka* and *Dhammapada* (Ahir 1994: 10) In other words, Ambedkar's Buddha is not a politically expedient fiction.

Let us now turn to the centerpiece of the Buddha's teaching, namely *prajna*, or understanding. Ambedkar presents the Buddha as giving permission to ordinary men and women, regardless of their station, to trust their experience over the authority of the learned Brahmins encoded in the Vedas and the Upanishads. But at the same time, the Buddha encourages them not to treat even their own experience, at any time, as infallible and exempt from revision. As against the unchanging cosmic order of the Vedas and the Upanishads, the Buddha taught that *everything* is always changing and there is no continuous and coherent self that experiences an unchanging reality. To cling to the idea of permanence is the source of suffering, while cultivating an attitude of 'mindful contemplation' of the ever-changing reality is the way to master and overcome suffering. Ambedkar interprets mindfulness to mean that 'everything must be open to re-examination and reconsideration, whenever grounds for re-examination and reconsideration arise' (*Dhamma*, 89). A re-examination, backed by 'logic and proof', and conducted with a spirit of 'freedom of thought', will itself change what the inquirer will value: not the certain knowledge of ultimate reality, but reliable knowledge of here and now. The Buddha (like Dewey) offers a method, not a doctrine, as a source of enlightenment.

Ambedkar presents the Buddha's own renunciation and Enlightenment as nothing more than an exercise in *prajna*, with nothing pre-ordained or divine about them. In Ambedkar's retelling, Siddharth Gautama, the son of the chief of Shakyas, a Northeastern hill-tribe, turns his back on his family and on his tribe not as a fulfillment of a pre-ordained fate, as the Buddhist lore would have it, but as a conscientious objector to his caste duties. He prefers to renounce the world, than follow his duty as a prince which demanded that he fight a war against a neighboring tribe. Ambedkar depicts him leaving home not in the dead of the night, stealthily, but openly, with a public affirmation of his pacifism, and in full consultation with his wife and his family. Not finding any of the existing philosophies helpful in explaining the cause of social conflict and suffering that he finds all around him, the young Siddharth resolves to 'examine everything for himself', to hold nothing as infallible and permanent, including the Vedas (58).

First thing the novice renouncer looks for is a new way of understanding that will help him discover the source of sorrow. He wanders from *guru* to *guru*, learning the traditional practices of penance, meditation and asceticism, only to declare 'this is not the way to passionlessness, nor to perfect knowledge, nor to liberation' (67). He stops mortifying his body, eats the famous bowl of rice pudding, and through 'reason and investigation', aided by 'concentration… equanimity and mindfulness' (75) achieves Enlightenment. His Enlightenment, in Ambedkar's retelling, amounts to discovery of a method by which to conquer the ignorance, the cravings and the hatreds that hold humanity in thrall.

In his first sermon at Sarnath, Ambedkar has the Buddha proclaim a rough paraphrase of the pragmatic maxim as a centerpiece of his Middle Path: 'you may ask, ye Parivrajatkas, why are these principles [of the Path of Purity] worthy of recognition as a standard of life', the Buddha asks. 'The answer to this question you will find for yourself if you ask, 'are these principles good for the individual? Do they promote social good?' (123). This leads him to fashion a crude pragmatic maxim: if it makes no difference to our experience, it is meaningless (257). The Buddha applies this rough and ready pragmatism to deny the existence of god, the immortal individual soul (*atman*) and universal soul (*Brahma*), and all supernatural forces (book III, part IV). Repeatedly, the Buddha refuses to answer any question about metaphysical matters, finding them 'not tending to edification' (270). But the answers he does favor – those amenable to logic and proof, and those that also promote human well being – help him to radically redefine all the major conceptual categories of Hinduism of his time: purity (which simply becomes 'good conduct,' p.229), *nirvana* (which becomes 'control over passions through knowledge and understanding' p. 234), dharma ('energetic action' 239), soul ('consciousness emerging from matter,' 262). If there is one single commandment that the Buddha issues to his followers, it is to accept nothing – not even his own teachings – if it does not accord with reason and experience. This commandment recurs repeatedly, like a mantra, right through Ambedkar's *Dhamma*.

Ambedkar's most touching – and to some most controversial – reinterpretation remains that of the doctrine of karma. Buddhism rejects the idea of immortality of the soul, but accepts the idea of rebirth according to the laws of karma, which do not essentially differ from those of Hinduism. In the traditional Buddhist writings, the soul is simply replaced by unidentified immaterial constituents which carry over the traces of karma into the next birth. Thus, 'even though Buddhism rejects the existence of the soul, this makes little difference in practice, and the more popular literature of Buddhism, such as the Birth Stories (*Jatkas*) takes for granted the existence of a quasi soul which endures indefinitely' (de Bary 1958, 92).

But Ambedkar seized upon this contradiction and asked: how can there be rebirth if there is no soul? Rather than take the traditional interpretations at face value, Ambedkar applies the

Buddha's own pragmatic maxim to the contradiction. He argues that 'if there is anything that can be said with confidence [about the historical Buddha] it is: He was nothing if not rational, if not logical. Anything, therefore, which is rational and logical, other things being equal, may be taken to be the word of the Buddha (351). Going by this interpretive principle, Ambedkar assumes that the Buddha would, if he could, agree with the findings of modern science. Thus we find Ambedkar committing the worst kind of presentism: he brings in the laws of Mendelian genetics and the laws of conservation of matter and energy to argue that karma cannot be inherited in the absence of the soul, and that all that is reborn is matter (329–344). Denying the immortality of the soul, Ambedkar interprets the Buddha as saying, you have to deny karma and rebirth, the latter decided by the karmic account of the soul's journey through all the past lives. Denuded of its metaphysics, and contained strictly within one lifetime, karma simply becomes another name for humanism that in the 'moral order rests on man's own actions and not on anyone else' (243).

There is ample evidence that Ambedkar's turn to Buddhism was not a matter of political expediency: passages from *Dhamma* clearly show how deeply moved he was by the Buddha's humanity and kindness. But it is equally clear that Ambedkar is keen on finding and foregrounding the social message of the Buddha. Thus *prajna* held a deeply political meaning for Ambedkar: it was the necessary first step toward the creation of a 'religion of principles' which free, equal and self-respecting people could practice, as against the 'religion of rules' which divides people, makes them cower in fear of unseen powers and robs them of an 'associated life' in the public sphere. Like Dewey in *A Common Faith*, Ambedkar is seeking to separate the religious attitude (the religion of principles) from its institutional trappings (the religion of rules). *Prajna* allows him to equate 'the cleaning of the mind as the essence of religion' (105): a genuine religious attitude becomes simply to act mindfully, to act with consciousness and responsibility and not obey any rules laid out in advance.[26] He seems to believe, perhaps too optimistically, that once reason becomes the basis of a new morality, equality (*samata*) and empathy/love (*karuna*) will follow. He had the Buddha's example before him. In a revolutionary break from the Brahmanical culture of his time, which limited access to the knowledge of Upanishads to a selected few, the Buddha made no distinctions of caste, class or gender. All were welcome to join his *sangha* (order) – and all came.

5. The Significance of Ambedkar's Buddha

> *If you meet the Buddha, kill the Buddha.*
> A Zen Buddhist commandment.[27]

Ambedkar's attempt to use the Buddha as a nucleus for scientific temper and a secular civil religion in India is revolutionary in more ways than meet the eye.

If, as Ambedkar observed, 'the history of India is nothing but a mortal conflict between Buddhism and Brahmanism,'[28] then Brahmanism has had an upper hand in the civil society, down to the contemporary times. Ambedkar's turn to Buddhism is a valiant attempt to correct the imbalance. The new Buddhism, however, is not meant for neo-Buddhists alone. Its real significance lies in the challenge it poses to the cultural common-sense of the rest of the Indian society. In turning to the Buddha, Ambedkar is attempting to 'extend the reach of reason' into the moral sentiments of the Indian society at large, an Enlightenment-style *kulturkampf* that Amartya Sen (2000) has recently argued for. Like his hero John Dewey, and like the philosophes of the European Enlightenment, Ambedkar is trying to make science relevant not just for new technologies, nor even for a new body of facts about nature, but for bringing about a change in the mode of thinking of the whole of Indian society. He is seeking a reconstruction of the conscious and unconscious taken-for-granted answers to questions regarding right and wrong, natural and unnatural, place of humans in the cosmos, etc. Ambedkar's neo-Buddhism contains the seeds of Indian Reformation and Enlightenment rolled into one.

There is no doubt that a turn to Buddhism has given the ex-untouchables, especially those from Ambedkar's own Mahar community, a new self-confidence and a new culture, complete with less superstitious and simpler life-cycle rituals. Many autobiographical accounts (most recently, Moon, 2001) and sociological studies (contributions in Narain and Ahir, 1994) attest to the changes: replacing old idols, fasts and ceremonies with readings from *Buddha and His Dhamma* conducted by *anyone* with a short training as a Buddhist priest, an explosion of creative expression of new rationalist, humanist themes through song and poetry (Guru, 1997), and above all, a growing sense of self-worth and pride. According to Timothy Fitzgerald, a scholar of Japanese and Indian Buddhism:

> Buddhists have achieved a new identity, symbolized by their change of name. The new optimism is strongly connected to ideas about self-reliance, rejection of the old Hindu subservience and a rational approach to their own self-development (1994: 20).

But all is not well. The ex-untouchables have found the Buddha, but they have not yet killed the Buddha. As Fitzgerald's field-studies (1994), and also the important study by Burra (1996) clearly show, the change in identity is not necessarily accompanied by a change in worldview, especially among the lower-income, rural neo-Buddhists. Their 'village Buddhism' (Fitzgerald's term) tends to make new gods out of the Buddha and Ambedkar and fit them into the Hindu pantheon. Old Hindu forms of idol-worship, ancestor worship and even the ideas of purity and pollution, directed at castes 'lower' than themselves remain widespread. Fitzgerald finds that it is the more educated, politically mobilized minority among neo-Buddhists who take the scientific temper of the Buddhist teachings into their lives.

Given that in India, it is not the bourgeoisie, nor the industrial working classes (those fabled carriers of modernity), but the deprived *castes* who stand to gain the most from a cultural revolution,[29] it is not surprising that Ambedkar's message should have taken hold of the imagination of dalits (notwithstanding its thinness among the poorer sections.) Unlike in the West where the rising bourgeoisie took on the cause of the Enlightenment, the lower castes rallying under the flag of reason in India have no money, no institutional power, no social prestige. For this reason, Enlightenment in India requires a much greater input from secular intellectuals, than did similar movements in the 17th and 18th century Europe. Unfortunately, for a variety of complex historical reasons, mostly upper-caste secular intellectuals in India have had more sympathy either with the *anti-Enlightenment* strains of Western and indigenous social theory, or with the Enlightenment strains of Marxism which privileges class over caste relations. The necessary (although not sufficient) role of reason in bringing about a cultural revolution has not been fully appreciated by non-dalit, secular intellectuals.

Even while Indian scholars wrote anguished tracts on the 'orientalism' and 'violence' of modern science, they completely ignored Ambedkar's seamless fusion of the ideas of John Dewey, the quintessential Yankee puritan, and the Buddha, the quintessential Asian philosopher. Ambedkar's Deweyan Buddha is a resounding affirmation of the universality of human aspiration for more truthful knowledge of nature in the service of human flourishing. Of course, non-Western people value their own cultural values, but it is simply not the case that they do not simultaneously value value-freedom, as Sandra Harding contends. What those at the bottom of non-Western societies are searching for is not an affirmation of their cultural values, just because they are 'their own'. What they seek is an affirmation of those aspects of their inherited cultural values that can help them gain some critical distance – which is another name for value freedom – from the values that have kept them in bondage. The life and the teachings of the Buddha are a living example that there has always been a reserve of skepticism and critical rationality toward dominant traditions in India. And the Buddha-Dewey synthesis is a living example that the veritistic traditions of premodern cultures are perfectly commensurate with the goals and methods of modern 'Western' science.

But the significance of Ambedkar's contribution goes beyond merely dispelling the postcolonial angst. His seamless blending of Dewey and the Buddha prepares the ground for recovering the pragmatic and naturalistic traditions that lie buried under the mystical idealism of Brahmanical trends in Hinduism. Recovery of these traditions and demonstrating their philosophical continuity with modern science offers a criterion for separating the core of authentic naturalist, rationalist traditions in Indian cultural heritage, from the Hindu fundamentalists' sham claims of 'scientificity' of Vedantic monism/non-dualism (see Feuerstein et al, 1995 for a representative text).

Because the Buddha's pragmatism bears an uncanny resemblance with American pragmatism's anti-metaphysical bent, it may create a suspicion that it was smuggled into the Buddha's teachings by the America-educated Ambedkar. But there is good evidence that the historical Buddha was deeply influenced by anti-Vedic naturalist philosophies prevalent in pre-Buddhist India, that of Lokayata (literally, 'prevalent among the people') and Sankhya (literally 'reflection'), both of which had a strong anti-metaphysical and anti-Brahmanical bent. The non-Brahmin, lower-caste Lokayata philosophers were famous (or infamous, among the priestly castes) for insisting upon putting the teachings of the Vedas, including all the rituals and spells meant to bring about a desired result, to a 'test of practice' in everyday life. For the Lokayata 'that alone is true which proves itself to be so in practical life' (Chattopadhyaya 1976:235). Like their contemporaries in Athens before Socrates, the Lokayatas denied any notion of a self (i.e. consciousness or *atman*) over and above the material body, saw all consciousness as an attribute of matter itself, and tried to explain all observed phenomenon by natural laws: they admitted no God, no soul, no survival after death. It has been established that references to Lokayatas, both in positive and in critical vein, abound in early Buddhist texts (Chattopadhyaya 1959: 47), including a quaint story of a skeptic who tried to detect 'a soul leaving a body by weighing the body before and after death'!

Likewise, there is evidence that Siddharth Gautama, before his Enlightenment, had studied with Sankhya philosophers in his own hometown. [30] The *original* Sankhya philosophy accepts non-sentient matter (*prakriti*) as the only and the first cause of all of nature, including sentience or consciousness (*purusha*) (Chattopadhyaya 1959: 381). Like the Lokayata, Sankhya too holds that the regularities and laws of *prakriti* can be understood through evidence of experience in here and now. This position is in stark contrast to that of the idealistic monism of Upanishads, which treats the *purusha* or the spirit as the first cause of all of nature, the latter having a status of mere illusion. True knowledge, the only kind of knowledge worth pursuing, according to these Brahmanical doctrines, is that of *purusha*, which being a part of the Absolute divine consciousness is declared to be beyond the grasp of all mundane experiences of ordinary mortals. [31]

Thus, the pragmatism that Ambedkar highlights in the Buddha was always there in the Indian intellectual history. *But – and this is crucial – it was always there as the repressed and the despised 'other' of the true, transcendental knowledge of the Brahmins.* Time and time again, the mystic idealism of Brahmanism has ridiculed, absorbed and in other ways demoted the empirical, experimental understanding of nature as *avidya* or false knowledge before the transcendental knowledge of the spirit: 'Gods love the mystic', the *Satapatha Brahmana* taught, 'Gods are fond of the obscure and detest direct knowledge.' The available historical texts tell the grim tale of the victory of Brahmanism: all that we know of Lokayata comes from the scorn and ridicule that was heaped upon it by the exponents of Vedanta; Sankhya was forced to compromise with Brahmanism by gradually making consciousness (*purusha*) the cause of nature (*prakriti*) and by re-introducing thoroughly un-Buddhist metaphysical questions into the later Buddhism (Chattopadhyaya 1976 and Dasgupta 1969). Transcendental knowledge, because it transcends mundane experiences accessible to ordinary people, remained strictly elitist. Indeed, the word Upanishads literally means 'secret knowledge', which was strictly denied to the unclean, 'once-born' castes.

The ideal of mystical over mundane, pragmatic knowledge has not changed much, even after India's encounter with modern science. Underneath the thin veneer of modernity in the public sphere, the traditional cultural codes survive in the private sphere and are gaining a new visibility even in the institutions of the state, schools and universities, the media, the police. (In April 2001 India officially instituted 'Vedic astrology' as a scientific discipline in colleges and universities.) Psycho-social (Kakar, 1981; Roland, 1988) and ethnographic (McKean, 1996) studies show high popular respect for mystical, magical knowledge of god-men, which is treated as the *really* real knowledge, as compared to the knowledge gained through ordering, categorizing and logical reasoning, as exemplified by scientists. Whereas the West rediscovered the naturalistic elements of its Greek heritage during the Renaissance and the Enlightenment, the Orientalist representations of India as essentially spiritual, combined with anti-colonialism led Indian nationalists to declare Vedantic idealism itself as a source of a more holistic science, superior in wisdom and insight than the 'reductionist' science of the West, a tendency that gained state backing under the Hindu nationalist government. At no point in modern Indian history, have the fundamentally nature- and reason-denying assumptions of Vedanta been critically examined.[32] The trend in the last two decades, as discussed in section 1, has been to embrace the wholism of Brahmanical thought which – in a complete falsification of the actual history – is made to stand in for the standpoint of women and the oppressed.

It is this context that makes Ambedkar crucial for a refutation of the feminist and postcolonialist case for an alternative epistemology. True, a non-separation between subject and object, between body and mind, between reason and emotions is held up as an ideal in Indian traditions. But this is the ideal of Brahmanical Hinduism which has legitimized the oppression of countless generations of men and women. True, the worldview derived from modern science is incommensurate with the basic axioms of the Hindu worldview which gives primacy to consciousness as the creator and the mover of matter. But this is the worldview that has for centuries discounted the ordinary sensory experiences of ordinary men and women and kept them in ignorance.

As his seamless weaving of modern science and the teachings of the Buddha shows, Ambedkar saw no incommensurability between the nature-endorsing and reason-affirming aspects of ancient Indian traditions and the ethos of modern science. He saw modern science only as a refinement and development of these nearly forgotten materialist and pragmatic traditions of the non-priestly, laboring castes in India. His Deweyan Buddha was a symbol of the unity of human reason and its still unfulfilled potential.

6. Conclusion

It is obvious that the postmodern skepticism regarding modern science completely disarms and delegitimizes Ambedkar's project. The only option for the friends of the oppressed in the postcolonial world – as the feminists and postcolonial intellectuals surely are – is for them to recognize that the interest of the oppressed in secularization and demystification of traditional ideologies is best served by the naturalism and skepticism of modern science. It would be fair to say that modern science *is* the standpoint of the oppressed.

Notes

1 An earlier version of this paper has appeared in *Social Epistemology*, 2001, vol. 15 (4): 335–365. Printed here with permission.

2 160 million men, women and children—nearly one-sixth of India's one billion people—belong to castes (jatis) which are considered occupationally, ritually and inherently polluted. India's Constitution makes untouchability illegal, but the practice still prevails. For the state of dalits in contemporary India, see Human Rights Watch, 1999. The website http://www.ambedkar. org is another valuable resource for Ambedkar's writings, as well as commentaries by dalit intellectuals.

3 Eleanor Zelliot, the American scholar of dalit movements, goes the farthest in exploring Ambedkar's American experience. But even she gives it very little importance: 'American influence on Ambedkar really counted for very little. It is more likely that in those early years in America, his own natural proclivities and interests found a healthy soil for growth …and strengthened him in his lifelong battle for dignity and equality of his people' (1992: 85).

4 For a overview of dalit intellectual activity, with a strong expression of concern with postmodernist tendencies, see Guru and Geetha, 2000.

5 By now there is a large volume of critical literature that argues that the Nietzschean, postmodernist reading of Dewey made popular by Richard Rorty in his *Mirror of Nature* (1979) does not capture the spirit of Dewey or the rest of the pragmatists. Indeed, Rorty himself has acknowledged that his postmodernist Dewey is a 'hypothetical Dewey', and an 'imaginary playmate', who says the sort of things Dewey would have said had he made the linguistic turn (Westbrook 1998: 128). See also, Haack (1998) for a critique of Rorty.

6 For all her critique of standpoint epistemology, Longino agrees with Harding's argument for strong objectivity. The transformative interrogation by scientific community that Longino uses as her shield against subjectivism will not prevent "community values to remain embedded in scientific reasoning" (Longino 1990: 216).

7 Important statements of epistemic charity can be found in Hess 1995; Turnbull 1997; Harding 1998.

8   Harding believes that a "woman scientist is a contradiction in terms", (1986: 59). "Women of color" is a "cyborg" identity made of all those "refused stable membership in the social categories of race, sex and class" and joined only by its "oppositional consciousness" to Enlightenment humanism (Haraway, 1991: 156).

9   The recent crop of overviews of the state of feminist science studies holds the bridging of subjectivity and objectivity as the distinguishing feature of feminist thought. See Code, 1998; Hirshmann, 1997; Harding, 2000.

10   This is a composite argument, made of many strands. The *locus classicus* for the Marxian strand is the work of Nancy Harstock and Sandra Harding, cited in the text. The psycho-analytical strand derives largely from Nancy Chodrow's 1978 classic, *Reproduction of Mothering*. Chodrow's object-relations theory was introduced into feminist epistemology by Evelyn Fox Keller (1982). The central text for the epistemic privilege of non-Western women is Vandana Shiva's *Staying Alive*. Also important are the writings of Sandra Harding (1998) and Fredrique Marglin (1996).

11   Kuhn (1977) singled out accuracy, simplicity, internal and external consistence, breath of scope and fruitfulness as values that scientists use to guide their judgment between competing theories.

12   Longino has progressively loosened the constraints of the existing community standards. In a 1993 publication, she argued for "detaching scientific knowledge from consensus" (1993: 114) in order to make room for critical oppositional positions in mainstream science. In that paper she proposed that different "sub-communities" in a given domain of inquiry be allowed to bring in their own models and metaphors that will allow them to "map" the relations posited in these models onto some portion of the experienced world. This "model theoretic theory of theories" was meant to allow different sub-communities to come up with different and incompatible maps of a domain that serve different and incompatible aims, without seeking consensus regarding one true story (1993: 116–117).

     In a bow to pluralism, Longino does not demand that the background assumptions/heuristic models of various "sub-communities" should have passed through the social process of transformative criticism that she admits is the hallmark of science. It can be readily shown that many of the models and metaphors of sub-communities she herself allows in her later work (e.g. ecofeminists) have never faced the tribunal of transformative criticism she holds as necessary for ensuring objectivity in science. Yet, all of these are to be admitted as feminist and alternative epistemologies.

13   Mosse (1961) for the influence of theosophy and the occult on Nazism.

14 Quoted here from Zelliot (1994). Namdeo Dhasal, a well-known dalit poet, is one of the founding members of Dalit Panthers, a militant dalit organization founded in 1972.

15 Most of the converts, including Ambedkar, expressed a feeling of liberation and starting afresh after the conversion. See Ahir(1994).

16 Mass conversions continued until his death. The 1951 census lists merely 2,500 Buddhists in India. The number jumped to 3 million in the 1961 census, a 1,671 percent increase. Cited from Deliege (1999).

17 See for example the recent book-length biography by Gail Omvedt (1994) who places Ambedkar in the historical context of the rise of democratic movements on the subcontinent. See also the short but pithy chapter on Ambedkar in Deliege (1999), although Deliege seems to under-estimate the man's religious impulse.

18 Even though they did not give ideological support to caste, the British did not actively oppose it either. Under the pretext of respect for local religion and customs, the British allowed the Brahmin priests to define social norms. See Aloysius (1998) for an interesting analysis.

19 Temple entry was never Ambedkar's priority. He nevertheless went along and allowed temple entry movements to use his name and prestige because he thought such movements served to unify the dalits politically.

20 Gandhi's defense of caste as fundamentally good, but only corrupted at the extremes, has remained the hallmark of all Hindu revivalist movements, down to the Hindu nationalist BJP. Even some spiritually inclined 'alternative development' movements, which have won accolades for their development efforts, staunchly defend caste order as communitarian, even while they try to include the lower castes in their development projects. The well-known Swadhyaya movement of Pandurang Athavale is an example of this tendency. See Little, 1995.

21 Arvind Sharma (1988), a vigorous defender of neo-Hinduism, describes traditional Hindu explanations for widowhood and sati (widow immolation) as consequences of women's 'karmic crimes'.

22 At least two volumes (volumes 3 and 4) of his collected works are devoted to this study.

23 Omvedt (1994) is an excellent source for understanding Ambedkar in his historical context.

24 O'Hanlon describes how mostly Protestant missionaries found some elements of Protestantism, the 18th century Enlightenment and the developing sciences which challenged Catholicism useful in their critique of Hinduism, and introduced these ideas in mission schools. But to

their great chagrin, their Indian students used these ideas to reject both Hinduism *and* Christianity.

25 This is an enormously contentious issue. It is well-established that the 'untouchable' communities are not free from caste prejudice. Ambedkar's own Mahar caste, for instance, looked down upon the Mangs, a caste supposedly even more polluted. But, by and large, those at the lower end of caste hierarchy do not accept the karmic explanations of caste, which blame the victim for their innate pollution. This has led some to claim that the notions of karma and dharma are irrelevant for understanding the dynamics of caste and that untouchables have a separate, egalitarian culture of their own, unpolluted by Brahmanical categories of thought. But autobiographical accounts and closer anthropological studies show that lower castes may not use ideas of karmic pollution /purity to explain *their own* position, but they use these ideas to differentiate those lower than themselves, and to express their sense of honor and status. For an illuminating review of the debate and a balanced position which shows the ambiguity of the untouchables vis-à-vis hierarchy, see Deliege, 1999.

26 "Doing what is good by virtue of a rule, and doing good in the light of a principle are two different things. The principle may be wrong, but the act is conscious and responsible. The rule may be right, but the act is mechanical. A religious act may not be a correct act but must at least be a responsible act." *Annihilation*, 124.

27 From Karen Armstrong's *Buddha*. Armstrong's biography of the Buddha contains one of the most lucid and insightful description of his Enlightenment.

28 Quoted here from Omvedt. http://www. Ambedkar.org

29 I agree with Gail Omvedt that the worldview of caste is not merely super-structural, but plays a direct role in enforcing exploitation of labor. Omvedt writes: "if we realize that the caste system both constitutes units of struggle (castes or jatis) and that rules of hierarchy and domination are essential to their constitution, then *the lowest castes have an inherent interest not simply in rising in the system but in overthrowing it*" (1994: 31), italics added.

30 Sankhya originated in the same Northeastern region of the Indian subcontinent, now in Nepal, where the Buddha came from. Buddha's birthplace, a village called Lumbini, was located near the ancient town of Kapilvastu, the abode of Kapila, the original Sankhya philosopher. This same region is also home to other proto-materialist religions of mother right and *tantra*. Chattopadhyaya (1959) hypothesizes a pre-Aryan origin of these ancient naturalist philosophies.

31 For an illuminating exposition of all varieties of Indian idealism, see the classic work of Surendranath Dasgupta (1969).

32 The exceptions are two well-known Marxist historians, Debiprasad Chattopadhyaya and D.D. Kosambi, both of whom were deeply influenced by Joseph Needham and J.D. Bernal. But this tradition has run aground against the new 'radical' sociology of science. There is hardly any active research program in this pre-social constructivist tradition of science studies.

References

Ahir, D.C., (ed). 1997. *Selected Speeches of Dr. B.R. Ambedkar*. New Delhi: Blumoon Books.

Aloysius, G. 1998. *Nationalism Without A Nation In India*. New Delhi: Oxford University Press.

Ambedkar, Bhim Rao. 1936. *Annihilation of Caste*. Jalandhar: Bhim Patrika Publications.

——. 1992 [1957]. *The Buddha and His Dhamma. Writings and Speeches*, vol. 11. Bombay: Government of Maharashtra.

Armstrong, Karen. 2001. *Buddha*. New York: Lipper/Viking Books.

Barnes, Barry and David Bloor. 1982. Relativism, Rationalism and Sociology of Knowledge. In *Rationality and Relativism*, 21–47. Cambridge: MIT Press.

Berger, Peter. 1967. *The Sacred Canopy*. New York: Doubleday.

Chattopadhyaya, Debiprasad. 1977. *What is Living and What is Dead in Indian Philosophy*. New Delhi: People's Publishing House.

Chattopadhyaya, Debiprasad. 1959. *Lokayata: A Study of Ancient Indian Materialism*. New Delhi: People's Publishing House.

Code, Lorraine. 1998. Epistemology. In *The Blackwell Companion to Feminist Philosophy*. Edited by Alison Jaggar and Iris M. Young, NY: Blackwell.

Dasgupta, Surendra Nath. 1969. *Indian Idealism*. Cambridge: Cambridge University Press.

Datar, Chhaya. 1999. Non-Brahmin Renderings of Feminism in Maharashtra. *Economic and Political Weekly*, Oct. 9: 2964–2968.

De Bary, Theodore (ed.). 1958. *Sources of Indian Tradition*, Vol. 1. NY: Columbia University Press.

Deliege, Robert. 1999. *The Untouchables of India*. Oxford: Berg.

Dewey, John. 1955 [1938]. Unity of Science as a Social Problem. In *Foundations of the Unity of Science: Toward an Encyclopedia of Unified Science*. Edited by O. Neurath, R. Carnap and C.Morris, Vol. 1, Nos. 1–10. Chicago: University of Chicago Press.

——. 1955 [1930]. *What I Believe. In Pragmatism and American Culture*. Edited by Gail Kennedy.23–32. Boston: D.C. Heath and Co.

——. 1929. *Quest for Certainty*. New York: Minton, Balch & Co.

——. 1925. *Experience and Nature*. NY: Dover

——. 1934. *A Common Faith*. New Haven: Yale University Press.

Feurestein, George, Subhash Kak and David Frawley. 1995. *In Search of the Cradle of Civilization*. Wheaton, Il: Quest Books.

Fitzgerald, Timothy. 1994. Buddhism in Maharashtra: A Tripartite Analysis. In *Dr. Ambedkar, Buddhism and Social Change*. Edited by A.K.Narain and D.C. Ahir. Delhi: B.R. Publishing.

Geetha, V. and S.V. Rajadurai. 1998. *Towards a Non-Brahman Millennium: From Iyothee Thass to Periyar*. Calcutta: Samya.

Gellner, Ernest. 1899. *Plough, Sword and the Book: The Structure of Human History*. Chicago: University of Chicago Press.

Guru, Gopal and V. Geetha. 2000. New Phase Of Dalit-Bahujan Intellectual Activity. *Economic and Political Weekly*, Jan 15: 130–134.

Haack, Susan. 1998. *Confessions of a Passionate Moderate: Unfashionable Essays*. Chicago: University of Chicago Press.

Haack, Susan. 1993. *Evidence and Inquiry: Towards Reconstruction in Epistemology*. Oxford: Blackwell.

Haraway, Donna. 1991. *Simians, Cyborgs and Women: The Reinvention of Nature*. New York : Routledge.

Harding, Sandra. 2000. Gender and Science. In *The Routledge Encyclopedia of Philosophy*. NY: Routledge.

———. 1998. *Is Science Multicultural?* Bloomington: Indiana University Press.

———. 1986. *The Science Question in Feminism*. Ithaca: Cornell University Press.

Harstock, Nancy. 1999. *The Feminist Standpoint Revisited and Other Essays.* Boulder, CO: Westview Press.

Hekman, Susan. 1997. *Truth and Method: Feminist Standpoint Theory Revisited.* Signs, 22, 341–365.

Hess, David. 1997. *Science Studies: An Advanced Introduction.* New York: New York University Press.

———. 1997a. If You're Thinking of Living in STS: A Guide For The Perplexed. In *Cyborgs and Citadels: Anthropological Interventions in Emerging Sciences and Technologies.* Edited by G. Downey and J. Dumit, 143–164. Santa Fe, NM: School of American Research Press.

———. 1995. *Science and Technology in a Multicultural World.* New York: Columbia University Press.

Hirschmann, Nancy. 1997. Feminist Standpoint As Postmodern Strategy. *Women and Politics*, 18, 73–92.

Human Rights Watch. 1999. *Broken People: Caste Violence against India's 'Untouchables'.* NY: Human Rights Watch.

Ilaiah, Kancha. 1998. Toward the Dalitization of the Nation. In *Wages of Freedom: Fifty Years of the Indian Nation-State.* Edited by Partha Chatterjee, 267–291. New Delhi: Oxford University Press.

Kakar, Sudhir. 1981. *The Inner World.* New Delhi: Oxford University Press.

Keller, Evelyn F. 1982. Feminism and Science. In *Feminist Theory: A Critique of Ideology.* Edited by Nannerl Keohane, Michelle Rosaldo, Barbara Gelpi, 113–126. Chicago: Chicago University Press.

Kuhn, Thomas. 1977. *The Essential Tension.* Chicago: University of Chicago Press.

Laudan, Larry. 1996. *Beyond Positivism and Relativism.* Boulder CO: Westview Press.

———. 1984. *Science and Values.* Berkeley: University of California Press.

Little, J. 1995. Video Vacna: Swadhyaya and Sacred Tapes. In *Media and the Transformation of Religion in South Asia*. Edited by Lawrence Babb and Susan Wadley, 254–284. Philadelphia: University of Pennsylvania Press.

Longino, Helen. 1997. Interpretation Versus Explanation in the Critique of Science. *Science in Context*, 10: 113–128.

———. 1996. Cognitive and Non-Cognitive Values In Science: Rethinking the Dichotomy. In *Feminism, Science and the Philosophy of Science*, edited by Lynn H. Nelson and Jack Nelson, 39–58. Dordrecht: Kluwer.

———. 1995. *Gender, Politics and Theoretical Virtues*. Synthese, 104: 383–397.

———. 1993. Subjects, Power and Knowledge: Description and Prescription. In *Feminist Philosophies of Science. Feminist Epistemologies*. Edited by Linda Alcoff and Elizabeth Potter, 101–120. New York: Routledge.

———. 1990. *Science as Social Knowledge*. New Jersey: Princeton University Press.

Marglin, Fredreique. 1990. Smallpox in Two Systems of Knowledge. In *Dominating Knowledge: Development, Culture and Resistance*. Edited by Fredrique A. Marglin.

McKean, Lise. 1996. *Divine Enterprise: Gurus and the Hindu Nationalist Movement*. Chicago: Chicago University Press.

Moon, Vasant. 2000. *Growing up Untouchable in India*. New York: Rowman and Littlefield.

Mosse, George. 1961. The Mystical Origin of National Socialism. *Journal of the History of Ideas*. Vol. 22 (1): 81–96.

Nanda, Meera. 2001. We Are All Hybrids Now: The Dangerous Epistemology of Postcolonial Populism. *Journal of Peasant Studies*, 28(2), 162–186.

———. 2001a. The Doublespeak of Hindu Science. *The Week*. June 24: 37–38.

———. 1998. The Epistemic Charity of Social Constructivism of Science and Why the Third World must refuse the Offer. In *A House Built on Sand: Exposing Postmodernist Myths About Science*. Edited by Noretta Koertege, 286–312. New York: Oxford University Press.

Nandy, Ashis. 1988. *Science, Hegemony and Violence: A Requiem for Modernity*. New Delhi: Oxford University Press.

Nandy, Ashis and Shiv Visvanathan. 1990. Modern Medicine and its Non-modern Critics: A Study of Discourse. In *Dominating Knowledge: Development, Culture and Resistance*. Edited by Fredrique.A. Marglin and Stephen A. Marglin, 145–184. Oxford: Clarendon Press.

Narain A.K. and Ahir, D.C. (eds.) 1994. *Dr. Ambedkar, Buddhism and Social Change*. Delhi: B.R. Publishing Co.

Nigam, Aditya. 2000. Secularism, Modernity, Nation: Epistemology of the Dalit Critique. *Economic and Political Weekly*, Nov. 25: 2003–2009.

O'Hanlon, Rosalind. 1985. *Caste, Conflict and Ideology: Mahatma Jotirao Phule and Low Caste Conflict in 19th Century Western India*. Cambridge: Cambridge University Press.

Omvedt, Gail. 1994, *Dalits and the Democratic Revolution: Dr. Ambedkar and the Dalit Movement in Colonial India*. New Delhi: Sage.

Putnam, Hilary. 1992. *Renewing Philosophy*. Boston: Harvard University Press.

Putnam, Hilary and Ruth A. Putnam. 1990. Epistemology as Hypothesis. *Transactions of Charles S. Pierce Society*, 26: 407–433.

Rege, Sharmila. 1998. Dalit Women Talk Differently: A Critique Of Difference and Towards A Dalit Standpoint Position. *Economic and Political Weekly*, Oct. 31. WS 39–WS46.

Roland, Alan. 1988. *In Search of Self in India and Japan*. Princeton N.J.: Princeton University Press.

Sen, Amartya. 2000. East and West: The Reach of Reason. *New York Review of Books*, July 20.

Sharma, Arvind. 1998. *Historical and Phenomenological Essays*. New Delhi: Motilal Banarsidas.

Shiva, Vandana. 1988. *Staying Alive: Women, Ecology and Survival in India*. New Delhi: Kali For Women.

Singer, Milton. 1972. *When a Great Tradition Modernizes*. Chicago: Chicago University Press.

Turnbull, David. 1997. Knowledge Systems: Local Knowledge. In *The Encyclopedia of the History of Science, Technology and Medicine in Non-Western Cultures*, 485–490. Dordrecht: Kluwer.

Weber, M. 1946[1922]. Science as Vocation. In *From Max Weber: Essays in Sociology*. Edited by Hans Gerth and C. Wright Mills, 129–158. New York: Oxford University Press.

Westbrook, R. 1991. *John Dewey and American Democracy*. Ithaca: Cornell University Press.

——. 1998. Pragmatism and Democracry: Reconstructing the Logic of John Dewey's Faith. In *The Revival of Pragmastism*. Edited by M. Dicksetein, 128–140. Durham: Duke University Press.

Youzhong, S. 1999. John Dewey in China: Yesterday and Today. *Transactions of the Charles S. Peirce Society*, XXXV: 69–88.

Zelliot, Eleanor. 1994. New Voices of the Buddhists in India. In *Dr. Ambedkar, Buddhism and Social Change*. Edited by A.K. Narain and D.C. Ahir, 195–208. Delhi: B.R. Publishing Co.

——. 1992. *From Untouchable to Dalit: Essays on the Ambedkar Movement*. New Delhi: Manohar.

Breaking the Spell of Dharma
A Case for Indian Enlightenment[1]

I. What is Enlightenment?

A picture, they say, is worth a thousand words. I came across one such picture recently that speaks far more eloquently about the roots of the crisis of India's secularism than many a learned tome. I urge you, dear reader, to take a long hard look at this picture – and weep.

It is a black-and-white wire photo, first printed in *The Times of India* on September 14 , 1987 and reprinted in Lise McKean's recent book, *The Divine Enterprise: Gurus and the Hindu Nationalist Movement*. The picture shows a crude wooden platform, about five feet high, with an emaciated, half-naked and unkempt old man dangling one leg over the wall of the platform. Underneath stands a middle-aged man clad in all white, with his bowed head touching the foot of that leg dangling from the platform. The owner of the leg is a "holy man" by the name of Sant Devraha Baba of Vrindavan. The bowed head belongs to none other than Balram Jakhar, the speaker of the Lok Sabha. The representative-in-chief of the house-of-the-people of this, the secular-democratic Republic of India, touching the feet of this alleged god-man with his forehead, seeking his blessings.

This picture troubles me. I wince every time I see it. Why? Haven't I seen it all before? Aren't utterly humiliating, hierarchical and non-reciprocal gestures of self-effacement before power – sacred and profane, in private and in public institutions alike – a routine part of social life in India? But the very fact that such sights are so commonplace, and that we have continued to accept them as facts of life, is exactly what troubles me. Indeed, the banality, the utter taken-for-grantedness of our elected representatives, in their official capacities, bowing, prostrating and in other ways displaying their helplessness and inferiority before religious authorities ought to trouble all secularists.

I read these displays of public religiosity as *signs of a democracy under the spell of dharma* – a democracy without democrats, a secularism without secularists. Unfortunately, whatever little discomfort we felt at such sights is fast disappearing: we do not even play at being secularists any more. Instead, elected representatives bowing before sadhu-sants is being touted as the Hindu ideal of *dharma rajya* where "the Rishis, through the authority of dharma, have the right to remove a king who defaults on his duty", where "dharma is higher than both the legislature and the judiciary", (Upadhyay, 1965). Reality has caught up with our schizophrenic national culture: we no longer profess to be secular in public and intensely religious in our private affairs; we now indulge in conspicuous religiosity in both public and private spheres. What is more, we claim that it is good thing too![2]

Move now, for a moment, from the late 20th century India to 18th century Europe. In 1763, Geneva's ecclesiastical assembly ordered one Robert Covelle to genuflect and listen to a reprimand for having fathered an illegitimate child. Covelle refused to kneel and turned to Voltaire, the leading light of the French Enlightenment, for help. Voltaire was outraged at the idea of religious authorities daring to *make a citizen kneel*: "An ecclesiastical assembly that presumed to make a citizen kneel would be playing the part of a pedant correcting children, or of a tyrant punishing slaves", Voltaire wrote in a pamphlet against genuflection. The rest of the *philosophes* rallied behind Voltaire, and after six years of agitation, succeeded in having genuflection abolished in Geneva (Gay, 1959, 63).

It is of numerous such refusals to kneel before authority that a public sphere worthy of a secular, liberal democracy is created. Because the "ecclesiastical authority" is dispersed, localized and self-enforced in our society, it calls for many more – not fewer – refusals. Where are the million mutinies that we need, everyday, at every level to create a society where no one can dare demand, or expect, citizens, or citizens' representatives, to kneel? Where is the outrage against the everyday tyrannies, fears and inhibitions perpetrated in the name of dharma that make our social institutions unfit for a free, equal and democratic people? Where are our Voltaires? Or is the impulse that propelled Voltaire and the rest of the members of the "Party of Humanity" to take up the cause of critical reason in the service of an open society, a "Western" impulse, inapplicable to India where religion is a "total way of life," a matter of "innocent" faith that cannot be questioned without losing the essence of being Indians?

A society where citizens do not kneel before authority of the Church and the State[3] did not emerge in the West without a protracted struggle against the *cosmopolis* sanctified by the church and traditions. The secularist doctrines of separation of church and state and the liberal idea of Rights of Man did not suddenly appear in the 17th and 18th century Europe, fully formed, either as unintended "gift of Christianity", or as an expression of "cultural genes" coding, some special Western propensity for freedom and individual conscience, as the culturalist from both the West and non-West alike like to claim. Nor was it an automatic unfolding of a universal law of progress, as vulgar materialists would have it. Instead, secularism in the West was an eminently political *achievement*. The liberal idea of rights-bearing individuals, including the right of conscience, had to be fought for against the medieval cosmology of Christianity, against all those institutions that embodied that cosmology, and against the classes whose privileges this worldview legitimated. In a sense, human rights, secularism and liberalism are "post-traditional" for they are objects of active effort and cannot be simply derived from any religious doctrine or metaphysics.

Yet, while cultural essentialism is false, *culture does matter*. Religious and cultural traditions – and the metaphysics they are rooted in – are not irrelevant to the content, breadth and depth of acceptance of post-traditional norms. Cultural traditions and religion *do* make a difference in how they either aid or impede the struggle for human liberty, equality and fraternity. Religious answers to questions of fundamental human importance – What the world is like? How has it come about? What makes us human? What is the goal of human life? How best to attain these goals and what errors to avoid? – constitute a kind of meta-reality or world-image which guide the social and ethical life of individuals, often at an unconscious level (Kakar, 1981). Different religious traditions differ in those elements of the meta-reality which make the idea of equal dignity of all human beings in here-and-now more, rather than less, easily acceptable.

Going against the grain of current trends in Indian sociology, which has either ignored or glorified the role of religion in Indian society, I will argue that there are elements of Hindu meta-reality – indeed, its central axioms of *dharma, karma* and *moksha* – which continue to impede the development of a liberal and secular civil society which respects the fundamental equality of right-bearing individuals. As the mere mention of the influence of Hindu worldview on social life in India raises red flags of "essentialism" or "orientalism", let me emphasize that I am not arguing that there is a single unchanging Hindu meta-reality which will always and forever over-ride the play of material interests, power, customary laws, other local traditions in society. All I am suggesting is that the multitude of local social institutions in India have had to engage with the central axioms of Brahmanical Hinduism, which have set the standards of all that is deemed ideal and desirable, even for those castes and sects of Hindus who do not actually live by these ideals: even the aspiration to achieve these ideals (as in Sanskritization), to construct an identity explicitly in defiance of these ideals (as in "Dalitization") is an indication of the power of these ideals. The "little traditions", and their customary laws cannot be adequately understood without understanding their relationship with the "Great traditions" of Brahmanical Hinduism, for the former gain their ethical bearings, their sense of right and wrong, from the latter. It is as sources of ideological hegemony, and not as the ultimate, unchanging motor of Indian history, that the content and uses of the central philosophical concepts of Hinduism bear a serious and critical examination.

While cultural meta-reality exerts a powerful influence on the structure of feeling, thinking and relating to nature and society, this meta-reality is *not* beyond rational examination and critique. A powerful case for the "reach of reason" into our sentiments and attitudes has been recently stated by Amartya Sen (Sen, 2000). In a response to those who would rather depend upon the supposedly spontaneous human emotions and the goodness of basic human instincts, than on supposedly cold and harsh light of reason and analysis, Sen argues forcefully that the inner world of unconscious fears and affects can be "influenced and cultivated through reasoning". Citing Adam Smith's *The Theory of Moral Sentiments*, Sen argues that even our instinctive reactions to particular conduct rely on "our reasoned understanding of causal connections between conduct and consequence…[and that] our first perceptions may also change in response to critical examination …" Lest one takes such propensity for critical examination to be a uniquely Western cultural trait, Sen provides an interesting reading of Akbar's insistence on exposing prevailing attitudes and social norms to critical reasoning. As I will argue throughout this paper, it is this continuous, open and rational critique of a culture's meta-reality, including its affective reality, and *not* some relativist gender, class or caste-indexed "epistemology of the oppressed" that best serves the interests of the oppressed.

Indeed, Sen provides a useful framework to understand the Enlightenment as that period in European history when the reach of critical reason extended into the meta-reality of the age. The 18th century Europe saw many changes in social manners, modes of address, assembly and social discourse, all increasing the level of civility and egalitarianism in everyday discourse in the public sphere. These changes in social manners were the outward signs of a *fundamental change in temper that questioned the validity and methodology of the knowledge of the natural world inscribed in myth, theology and inherited traditions.* If there was one single passion that defined the 18th century Enlightenment – that "revolt against superstition," as Kant called it – it was a passion for critical reason in the service of demystification of church doctrines, supernatural beliefs, miracles and other such magical-religious practices. The network of otherwise quarrelsome *philosophes* that extended from France, England, Holland and Germany to the Americas, drew its sense of purpose from a belief in the redemptive power of new ways of knowing the world. The new philosophy of knowledge was exemplified above all by Newton's great success, and given a philosophical expression by John Locke's empiricism. It demanded publicly testable evidence based on experience and reason, the *natural capacity of which is equally available to all,*[4] demolishing all claims of *a priori* knowledge available only to select few through the grace of god or through their privileged social status. Of course, all people, all societies, at all times, reason, and reason critically, as the critics of Enlightenment like to point out. But the Enlightenment marks a culmination of a process that, through Renaissance, the Reformation and the Scientific Revolution and propelled by the forces of nascent capitalism, revolutionized *what reason meant* and what role it had in how men and women related to nature and to each other. "The purpose", wrote Diderot, the author of the *Encyclopedia*, the remarkable compendium of the European Enlightenment, "is not only to supply a certain body of knowledge, but also *to bring about a change in the mode of thinking*" (quoted from Cassirer, 1951, p. 14).

This "change in the mode of thinking" lay broadly in a change from a contemplative, deductive reasoning from intuitively-grasped, god and tradition sanctioned *a priori* beliefs to an insistence on deriving any claim regarding nature's order from the data of experience alone. Knowledge was no longer to proceed from concepts and axioms to phenomenon, but vice versa. At its core, the Enlightenment was an attempt to popularize and institutionalize modest procedural principles of knowledge that insisted on breaking apart all existing claims of cause and effect derived from earlier metaphysical systems and rationalist schemes, and to test them against observation and experiment. If there was a dogma of Enlightenment, it was that there were to be no dogmas, no *a priori* truths and no privileged Sources of Affirmation. All dogmas could be queried by private citizens, who have the right to come together in the public sphere, as equals, to pursue truth through open critical debate.[5] Needless to say, in actual practice, these ideals were marred by myriad inequities of class, gender and citizenship. The *philosophes* themselves were not free from what we would today reject as grossly elitist prejudices. But an exclusive, hyper-critical concern with these contradictions can blind us to the momentous implications of winning public legitimacy for new norms for public reason. These more democratic, naturalistic and secular norms were, in time, to expand to take in the excluded segments of society, leading both toward a more egalitarian *and* simultaneously a more rationalized, instrumental society.[6]

Such a change of temper toward nature, knowledge and society was not an automatic response to the change in material conditions

– rising literacy, growing affluence, increasing class mobility – associated with the coming of industry and capitalism. It is a mistake, commonplace in Marxist writings, and unfortunately in Marx's own writings,[7] to reduce the Enlightenment's view of rights and negative freedoms to an expression of purely material, class interests of the bourgeoisie. This is a serious misunderstanding of the Enlightenment, both because it fails to do justice to the actual concerns that motivated the rising middle classes of the 18th century Western Europe, especially France, and because such a narrow materialist reading does not allow one to look for homologues of the European Enlightenment in non-European societies. As we shall see in the course of this paper, a class analysis fails to understand the Indian Enlightenment which, I will contend, finds its intellectual and political motivations in the quest for recognition of their humanity by the oppressed castes, *as castes*, rebelling not merely for their material/class interests, but against the social and existential insults heaped upon them. A purely economic motivation does not explain the hard-fought battle in the cultural realm against the dogmas of the age.

The Enlightenment's call for reason at the service of "Liberty, Equality and Fraternity" is best understood as a call to arms in a *struggle for recognition* of equal dignity of all, regardless of origins and station in life. The Enlightenment counterposed the idea of honor in the *ancien regime* with that of dignity: whereas for some to have honor, it was necessary that not everyone has it, the underlying principle of dignity is that everyone shares in it by the virtue of being human (Taylor, 1992). Seen in purely class terms, the interests of the bourgeoisie in France – the flag-bearers of the French Enlightenment – were not all that different from the class interest of the nobility. Like the nobility, the rising middle classes of the Third Estate also aspired to accumulate proprietary wealth in land, office or rents, which involved a minimum of risk and could safely be handed down in the family. The capitalist entrepreneur, speculating with borrowed capital and few fixed assets was not typical of the upper middle classes. What the well-heeled bourgeoisie resented was not much economic frustration, as social disparagement at the hands of the nobility which claimed to derive its status from lineage. The rising bourgeoisie were motivated not by a desire to revolutionize the economic basis of society but to dismantle those social ideologies and attitudes that denied them full recognition of their own worth. Not just in France but in most of Europe, the 18th century bourgeois revolutions were struggles waged between relatively well-off minorities – "a revolt of the privileged", as Norman Hampson (1969) calls it – with hardly anyone contemplating the full enfranchisement of the urban and peasant masses.

The fundamental ideas of the Enlightenment philosophers – reason as a distinguishing mark of humanity and a basis for entitlement to equal respect, and nature as devoid of divine purpose and hierarchy and amenable to human understanding and control – struck a chord with the bourgeoisie. These ideas enabled them to challenge the superstitious acceptance of the prevailing order personified by the priests and the king. Man was henceforth, at least in theory, to be free to create for himself the social and political conditions necessary for his own development. True this "man" was cast in the image of white, male and bourgeois man. But the underlying conception of reason and nature of the Enlightenment contained within it the seeds for its own self-universalization. In time, the Enlightenment philosophy has been embraced by not just the labor movement but all those – including the suffragists, black liberation and anti-colonial movements – seeking liberal political reforms (Bronner, 1995).

European Enlightenment did not emerge out of the shadowy mists of Western culture or traditions. This movement was deliberately created and set in motion by human beings at a definite point in time, on the basis of a certain theoretical understanding of man and nature. Neither the Protestant Reformation of the 16th century,[8] nor the Scientific Revolution of the 17th century,[9] alongside the growing forces of industrial capitalism,[10] were sufficient for bringing about the displacement of myth and god from social life. It took the principled intervention of public intellectuals of the emerging pan-Euro-American "Republic of Letters" – journalists, pamphleteers, science popularizes, amateur scientists, mostly men but some women, some well-known and independently wealthy, others provincial and struggling – to spell out the philosophical and social implication of the advances in scientific knowledge. The great achievement of the Enlightenment was to build a political vision based upon reason, to transform reason from an arid epistemological position of interest to professional philosophers alone into a social ethic: the refusal to accept anything without demonstration and reason, was simultaneously a refusal to bow to the authority of those who have hitherto claimed a unique possession of truth.

II. The Enlightenment Project Under Fire

One of the most important jobs of intellectuals, whether as priests, philosophers or activists is to define what is wrong with their society, and to identify the obstacles that stand in the way to a desirable future. Identification and articulation of the causes of our social malaise generate new objects of desire, longing and hatred and new modes of social activism.

Through a strange and dangerous convergence of anti-imperialist/anti-capitalist and populist Third Worldist impulses in the second half of the 20th century, an influential segment of left academics and activists around the world have tended to *identify the legacy of the Enlightenment itself as an obstacle to a desired society.* The "progressive" discourse, among the heirs of Nietzsche, Gandhi and Marx alike, is characterized by a deep despair over the modern condition engendered by science-based industry, nation-states and increasingly global markets. The conditions of modern life are seen as deforming and dehumanizing individuals, by turning them into bourgeois, philistines and lost men. One discerns a deep "longing for total revolution" which will overcome the modern structure of feeling, thinking and acting (Yack, 1992), and lead to a more whole, less alienated modernity. This longing best explains why a certain image of "Reason" and "the Enlightenment" have become for the postmodern and postcolonial intellectuals what the *ancien regime* was to the Enlightenment: an intimate enemy against which the critics define their own projects of "alternative modernities". The critics claim that it is in the interest of the oppressed to challenge the phony "objectivity" of science with their more "authentic" and holistic ways of knowing which, unlike modern science, do not tear apart nature from society, the object from the subject, facts from meanings, reason from affect etc. "Oppositional consciousness", it is claimed, must extend to an opposition to scientific world view and scientific reason itself.[11]

This urge to overcome the heritage of the Enlightenment poses a special set of problems for postcolonial societies where the Enlightenment project has not yet taken off the ground, let alone having allegedly reached a point where it has turned into its opposite. The desire for a total revolution is nothing less than a disaster for a society like India where cultural nationalism has allowed an illiberal and segmentary social logic, sanctified by the core assumptions of Hindu dharma, to continue to serve as a cultural code, even among the most secular and enlightened political and intellectual leaders.[12] Before the supposed communitarian, humane and rational elements, myth and traditions can be recovered – as the Gandhian neo-romantics desire – they must first be forced to loosen the deadly grip they have had for centuries on the Indian imagination. Before the liberal Enlightenment regime of economic and civic liberties can be radicalized – as the Marxists desire – they must first be allowed to win legitimacy over and against the dharmic common sense of the Indian society.

In India, different elements of postcolonial "left"-inclined intelligentsia have different conceptions of desirable futures in whose name Enlightenment is to be indicted. A word about my use of the appellation "left" when applied to intellectuals, activists and social movements may be appropriate here. What passes as "the left" in India today includes well-known personalities and social groups that I call "reactionary modernists". These groups are mostly associated with neo-Gandhian communitarians, who share the postmodernist and postcolonial suspicion of reason and the Enlightenment, but *not* the postmodernist critique of essentialism. Thus, while they accept the postmodernist idea of cultural embeddedness of all ways of knowing (which reduces modern science to a mere "ethnoscience" of the West), their view of "Indian mode" of knowing and relating is essentially a Hindu, non-dualist mode, and their view of Indian community is an idealized dharmic, wholist community.[13] (Can they be called "contingent postmodernists" or "strategic postmodernists"?). I call these intellectuals, including internationally acclaimed stars like Ashis Nandy, Vandana Shiva, Partha Chatterjee, Gayatri Spivak (in parts), Gyan Prakash, Dipesh Chakravarty, Veena Das, Claude Alvares and their numerous fellow travelers and followers, reactionary modernists because they seek to model their alternative modernities on the "innocent", "genuinely archaic" and supposedly subaltern modes of knowing and living, completely ignoring the fact that these same local knowledges are, more often than not, patently irrational, obscurantist and downright oppressive to the same subaltern on whose behalf these intellectuals claim to speak. Their *de facto* advocacy of Hindu tradition notwithstanding, these intellectuals retain an aura of progressive left politics because of their association with the classic left causes (anti-imperialism, multi-culturalism, feminism and environmentalism), although in my opinion, they are actually the bridge between the nationalist elements of the anti-capitalist left and the full-blown, fascist religious right.

The other component of the left is of course the organized Marxist left which has traditionally stood for a modernist socialist solution to overcoming the inequities and injustices of capitalism. But this stream of the Indian left, unfortunately, has allowed its economism to under-estimate the value of non-economistic struggle in the realm of culture and meaning that the Enlightenment was all about. The more traditional Marxist left has looked to an as yet unrealized socialist future where "true" critical reason and "true" human autonomy will be realized: Enlightenment and its supposed "positivism", "rationalism" and its supposed self-universalization stand indicted because of their historical connection with capitalism and imperialism.[14] The true potential of the Enlightenment, on this reading can only be achieved under socialism.[15] This appropriation of Enlightenment project for socialism constitutes a misreading of the actual history of the Enlightenment Europe where a *relative autonomy* of the public sphere from class interests allowed the institutionalization of procedural rationality in public affairs. There is no doubt that the Enlightenment shared the glorification of work, industry and the profit motive that marked the Protestant ethic of the rising capitalist class (Gay, 1977, 45–55). But it would be a mistake to reduce the Enlightenment to an ideology of capitalism and imperialism alone. As Jurgen Habermas' influential study of public sphere has shown, aristocrats, men of property and men of letters played a formative role in creating the institutions – salons, coffee houses, newspapers, journals of opinion– where "common interest in truth allowed 'bracketing' of status differences" (Calhoun, 1992, p. 13) in public discussions of a variety of topics ranging from the latest scientific discoveries to matters of religion and state. It is very likely that "common interest" was often a cover for class interests, and there is no doubt that the public sphere was restricted in its initial phase to only those who could afford the books, the public lectures and the coffee houses. But however often it was breached, the idea that the best rational argument, and not the identity of the speaker, was important to arrive at truth was gradually institutionalized as the norm for public discourse.

In an open society that admits of a plurality of interests, identities and self-chosen ends, it is important that the public sphere and the norms of discourse not be controlled and dominated by any one class interest: there is no "subject position", no unique "standpoint" of the proletariat, or dalits, or women or any chosen group that can liberate the whole of society. Public reason must be conceived of as a never-ending critical debate among contending interests where the content of the argument can be judged through publicly testable experience, independently of the class/caste/gender identity of the arguer. *That* is the essence of critical rationality that the Enlightenment project was all about, and not the sterile debates about "foundationalism" or "positivism" or "Eurocentricity". Marxist suspicion of universalizable claims of reason and experience which can transcend class interests have contributed to an underestimation of the importance of procedural rationality in social institutions; and conversely, the Marxist priority to material forces has led it to under-estimate the hold of the *dharmic* view of the world on social life and how it stands in the way of equal recognition of the humanity of each and every person, regardless of ascribed status. I intend a more thorough critique of the Marxist understanding of modern science and the Enlightenment in a future publication. This little detour is only meant to signal my dissatisfaction with Marxist alternatives to the anti-Enlightenment discourse so common in the indigenist, postmodernist movements.

If on the other hand, the Enlightenment is a struggle for recognition (see the previous section), it is not the Indian bourgeoisie, or the miniscule organized working classes but the *oppressed castes* who have been the most principled and consistent proponents of an Enlightenment-style critique of Brahmanical Hinduism, which provides both the conscious ideology of *varna dharma* and the everyday rules of behavior among and between castes.[16] The largely upper-caste Indian bourgeoisie have been more than willing to embrace an updated and sanitized neo-Hinduism as their worldview, for it allows them to stake out a claim for recognition from the West as members of a "Great Civilization" equal to, if not better than the civilization of their erstwhile colonizers. Thus, for all the formal gestures toward modern ideas of scientific temper, secularism and liberalism, political leaders and intellectuals have, by and large, understood these terms in a neo-Hindu, *dharmic* idiom.[17] In theory, there is nothing wrong with an attempt to seek indigenous-religious legitimation for modern ideas: indeed, finding cultural homologues and historical antecedents may be even necessary for a new modernist cultural ethos to develop and take root. But the problem is that *Hinduism, both in its principles and in its practices, directly contradicts the view of reason and nature that is necessary and adequate for a liberal polity and culture of the Enlightenment.* Given the peculiar nature of Hinduism, we in India cannot unproblematically turn to our dominant religious traditions in search for an anchor for modern ideas. We have no option but to create new traditions on the foundation of minority, anti-Brahmanical traditions that have been ridiculed and silenced for centuries. It is not only intellectually dishonest to read back secularism, liberalism, scientific temper – and even the most revolutionary findings of modern science – into the ancient "wisdom" of the Vedas, as neo-Hindus from Vivekananda, Gandhi, Radhakrishnan and even Nehru to some extent have done, and as the likes of Murli Manohar Joshi continue to do in our own times, or to argue for a specifically Hindu view of science ("ethno-science"), reason and nature, as the neo-Gandhian, "critical traditionalists" and postmodernists continue to do. Such sanitization of Hinduism or Hinduization of modernity is downright dangerous, for it absorbs and disarms all potential challenges to Hinduism and the illiberal, hierarchical worldview sanctioned by it.

Unlike the political Brahmanism of upper caste nationalists, who are satisfied with the reformist agenda of eradicating untouchablity but retaining the basic worldview and institutions of *varna-dharma,* the oppressed castes have an "inherent interest not simply rising in the system but in overthrowing it" (Omvedt, 1994, 31). Given the long and oppressive history of India's peculiar institutions, *the agents of "bourgeois revolution" in India will not be the bourgeoisie, but the poor and insulted castes,* for it is they who have experienced both the objective deprivation and the subjective insults of Hindu social institutions. These castes have natural allies among those segments of Indian society who have no interest in preserving the *ancien regime* and these include, above all, women of all classes and castes who have been deprived of their full agency and humanity by Hindu patriarchy. Because the "purity" of upper-caste women has been paid for by the enforced segregation of the men and women of "impure" castes (Chakravarti, 1993), women, together with the non-Brahman castes, share an objective interest in shaking the ideological pillars of Hinduism. Contrary to the exhortations of ecofeminists and cultural feminists, reason and science are allies of women in their joint struggle with the Dalits against patriarchy and caste.

Before I move on to the real purpose of this paper – which is to affirm the relevance of the Enlightenment project or what used to be called "scientific temper" in India – let me sum up my discomfort with the contemporary left opposition to the Enlightenment project. The left intelligentsia in India has looked at the Enlightenment through a bifocal lens: one "anti-materialist", which views the Enlightenment as perpetrator of Eurocentrism and Orientalism, leading to a "colonialism of the mind"; and the other "materialist" that sees it as the ideology of capitalists and imperialists. Both these lenses are equally distorting for they fail to see Enlightenment for what it was: a movement to change the way of thinking of a civilization. Capitalism and colonialism were *contingent* features of the Enlightenment: capitalism facilitated but did not determine the content of Enlightenment, whereas colonialism, as Robert Darnton has put it, " was driven by trade, disease, technology, rather than by philosophy". What was *necessary* to the Enlightenment was critical reason or scientific temper, captured by Kant's call of "*Sapere aude!* Have courage to use your own reason".

This essential core of the Enlightenment is as relevant to India today, as it was to Europe in the 18th century. Indeed, contrary to the critics, this essential core of Enlightenment is not a foreign import at all. The intellectual resources and political motives for critical reason, or "scientific temper", have been with us since the Lokayatas, which surfaced again, after centuries of suppression and ridicule by the Vedantists, in the naturalism, skepticism and pragmatism of Phule, Periyar and Ambedkar. These ideas took a bourgeois form in our time in the Nehruvian idea of "scientific temper". The call for scientific temper, even though couched in whiggish, Nehruvian terms and often conducted through a contemptuous, top-down development bureaucracy, was *not* contradictory to Ambedkar's call for reason in the service of "annihilation of caste. .Had it not been written off so hastily under the influence of neo-Gandhians and postmodernists, there was no reason why middle-class, left-inclined intellectuals and activists who swell the ranks of social movements could not have created working alliances with the inheritors of the Lokayatas among the rationalist Ambedkarites and self-respecters. After all, substantial number of these intellectuals and activists were already participating in people's science movements and were deeply engaged with science and development policies. A misguided, uneducated and pseudo-radical critique of critical reason and modern science, borrowed from the fashionable nonsense that prevails in some segments of the Western academe, has prevented the full flowering of a radical Enlightenment-style movement in India. The culturalist understanding of science and reason has diverted the people's science movements into indigenist and economistic critiques of imperialism, rather than a self- critique of dominant and oppressive traditions. The "reactionary modernism" of Hindutva is a direct beneficiary of the indigenist left's slide into irrationalism.

III. The "Science Wars" and Indian Science Critics

I am a child of the Enlightenment. Those irreverent, spirited, and courageous men and women of French salons, English coffee-houses, learned academies and public lecture-halls are my brothers and sisters in spirit. I came to share their heretical project long before I had ever heard their names, or read their works. My provincial, mid-middle class, Punjabi upbringing gave me good reasons to fight against the patriarchal, upper-caste Hindu traditions that threatened to snuff out all that I held precious. I had the motive for rebellion, but not the intellectual tools – until I encountered modern biology and physics which altered my view of the world entirely. It was the empowering influence of science that inclined me towards people's science movements and science journalism. The much trashed idea of "scientific temper" was not an "elitist" and "Western" fad for me, but a way of life and a philosophy for social action.

I have watched with great sorrow how modern science, scientific temper and Enlightenment have been repeatedly trashed by ever more "radical" intellectuals and activists, and how myth, traditions and "lived experience" have been elevated as the source of "liberatory" ethno-sciences. My sense of loss over these misguided critiques, however, began to turn into political concern with the rise of the Hindu right which has been the chief beneficiary of the erasure between myth and science.

This background should explain why I have taken on a difficult and personally costly battle on two fronts. First against the "theorists", located mostly but not solely in the West, who have produced sociological and philosophical arguments against the idea of a universal and progressive science of nature, and second, against the ready embrace of these relativist theories of science by Indian intellectuals. It so happened that around the time when I got started with my project, some working scientists and philosophers of science in the US, led by Paul Gross and Norman Levitt, a biologist-mathematician pair, also began to question the dominant paradigm of sociology of science, cultural studies and feminist critiques of science.[18] It was while the "radical" critics of science were trying to argue their way out of Gross, Levitt and associates' critique, that the now-famous Sokal hoax appeared. (The *Social Text* issue in which Sokal's contribution appeared was titled "Science Wars" and was meant to be a response to Gross and Levitt). My critique of social constructivism converged with what Gross and Levitt, and Alan Sokal were saying, even though I had not put the matter as glibly as the first two, or as creatively (!) as Sokal.[19]

The science wars in the US were noticed in India. A handful of Indian scientists and rationalists expressed their support for Sokal. In 1997, Alan and myself (along with Stephen Jay Gould) were invited by the Socialist Scholars Conference for a panel on science wars. The papers we read at that conference were published in EPW (April 18, 1998). These papers have provoked much criticism – as well as a great deal of sympathy. First Gita Chadha took up cudgels in defense of feminist epistemology and relativism (EPW, April and Aug. 1997, Jan. 1999), followed by Sundar Sarukkai (March 27, 1999) who made a detailed critique of my views on the nature of science, its cultural meaning and relevance for a critique of religious thought in India.

I stand guilty – and proudly so – of most of the sins Sundar Sarukkai accuses me of having committed in my defense of the "outmoded" idea of scientific temper. Not only do I hold the "absurd" view that "one ought to live science and not just do it", I even think – heavens forbid!—that without allowing the modern scientific worldview to serve as a cultural force in society, all the talk of "demolishing power structures" and "empowering the powerless" will go nowhere. I am guilty, as charged, of the "facile belief" that the *content* of our beliefs about the nature of "things" affects how we treat people, and that the *process* of arriving at these beliefs about things affects how we relate to authority in our private and public lives. I am guilty as well of not conceding parity between scientific explanations and local folk beliefs. I am guilty, in other words, of believing that through the 300-odd years since the scientific revolution, human beings have learnt how to learn better, and there is no reason why we should not expose our ancestral knowledge to what we have learned about the world through modern scientific methods. And of course, I am guilty, as charged, of not heeding the siren songs of postmodernism and postcolonialism. But does this litany of sins mean that I am also guilty of being "blind to the lived experience" of peasant women? Or that I see science as a substitute for real material changes in power structure? Or that I do not appreciate the real local causes in India for disillusionment with science and modernity and the consequent turn to postmodernism? Or that I am attacking Indian intellectuals from a position "more American than Americans"? These accusations I firmly reject.

I decided to continue a conversation with Sarukkai in this paper because he has raised truly fundamental questions regarding the relationship between *growth of knowledge of nature and the expansion of human capabilities and liberties*, or between the domains of "things" and "people", respectively, in Sarukkai's words. The very essence of Enlightenment lies in the belief that as we learn more about nature, and as we learn how to learn better, we also learn how to live without any transcendent authority, without a fear of the unknown and without fear of those who think differently. To go back to our earlier concern, *a society where citizens don't kneel before spiritual authority is possible only when we divest the natural world of final causes and ultimate ends determined by a super-mundane power and accessible only to some through the grace of god.*[20] How we understand nature and how we treat each other are not two different, and unrelated "domains, ,as Sarukkai treats them. Rather, a naturalistic, secular understanding of the domain of nature is a necessary precondition for a secular, democratic society to emerge.

The relationship between the domains of nature and the domain of society is absolutely basic – but also the most ignored – for understanding the radical potential of science and scientific temper in India. I am grateful to Sarukkai for bringing it up and I will use this opportunity to expound on it at various levels, ranging from everyday practices to the philosophical tenets of Hinduism.

IV. Restating the Case for Scientific Temper
(With Some Help from "Islam's Luther")

The first stop in our journey to find the rationale and resources for Indian Enlightenment will be Iran.

Why Iran? Iran of the Ayatollahs, at that? Because after two decades of living under theocratic rule, Iranian intellectuals are raising the banner of the Enlightenment. I am referring to the highly influential writings of Abdol Karim Soroush. Going by the fear and loathing he brings out in the religious establishment, and the adulation and enthusiasm he generates among the Iranian youth, Soroush is clearly one of the most influential public intellectuals of Iran today. A part of the Islamic establishment (until recently) *and* its most feared critic, a man of faith *and* a follower of Popper's philosophy of science, Soroush has been called the Martin Luther of Islam.

I will be honest. It is partly a sense of personal vindication that attracts me to Soroush: he is saying in a much more forceful way precisely what I and other much derided "rationalist secularists" have been saying all along. It is not out of place, therefore, that I should enlist his help in making my own views clearer.

Soroush's advocacy for democracy in Islam rests on two pillars. One, freedom as a precondition for true belief in Islam; and the second, evolution of human knowledge, i.e. science and its relevance to interpretation of *sharia* or the word of God. Soroush has argued his second principle at great length in his thesis on T*he Evolution and Devolution of Religious Knowledge* (Soroush, 1998).

His basic argument is simple and proceeds in two steps: "Religion is divine, but its interpretation is thoroughly human and this-worldly" and two, "[the interpretation of religion] is the natural product of the *evolution of human understanding in non-religious fields and contexts* that forces religion to be comprehended differently" (1998: 246, italics added). What Soroush is insisting upon is rather elementary but revolutionary: since the Scientific Revolution, scientific discoveries of the natural world have altered the humanity's knowledge of itself and its place in the world. This altered self-knowledge made possible by science must influence how we interpret the word of God, or the dogmas of religious thought, or any other sacralized practice. As a believer, Soroush is not arguing for an end to the religious impulse, but he is demanding *that this impulse become contemporaneous*, that is, it becomes contingent upon the pursuit of a systematic, methodical, rational and justifiable inquiry, best represented by modern science. As long as our understanding of the truth about nature is evolving, our interpretation of religion cannot stand still because religious knowledge, too, makes claims regarding the relationship between man, nature and society.

On the surface, the religious right and the proponents of ethnosciences seem to make similar arguments. For example, proponents of "Islamization of knowledge" including Ziauddin Sardar and his followers (Sardar, 1988) have long insisted that Islam is not a rigid dogma but allows sufficient interpretive flexibility within the limits of the core idea of unity of God (*tawhid*). Likewise, BJP-RSS writings on science (Feurerstein et al, 1995) celebrate the interpretive flexibility and modernity of Hinduism. As far as the demand that traditions do not contradict the rationality of science, both the religious right and the left anti-secularists re-define science to fit the native genius, and in turn, use these ethno-sciences as the benchmark of rationality of modern "Western" science – this is what the talk of "alternative universals" amounts to in practice. The Hindu right takes the left-indigenist argument to its logical conclusion and claims that norms of reason internal to High Hinduism are not only capable of producing special sciences indigenous to India (e.g. Vedic mathematics, Vedic physics, Vastu shastra, ayurveda etc.), but are in fact affirmed by, and presage, the findings of modern sciences. In the Hindutva scheme of things, to be scientific all that Indians – nay, the whole world – has to do is to come home to Vedic Hinduism!

Soroush is arguing for the exact opposite of the above position: not *Islamization of science*, but a *reinterpretation of Islam* in the light of science understood as a universally valid stock of justified beliefs about the natural world. His argument is not that science should replace religion, but only that the body of knowledge amassed by human intellect in the secular realm should be a guide for refining and developing man's understanding of the sacred. What separates Soroush from the nativists of both the Left and the Right is his *understanding of the nature of science*. Very simply, Soroush is a Popperian who believes in growth of objective knowledge, while the indigenists of all stripes embrace varying versions of social constructivist theories that deny the very idea of knowledge that is free from cultural values particular to a place, a people and a time. This is as good a place as any to clarify that those like Soroush, Popper, and many post-positivist philosophers of science who believe that objective knowledge is possible are *not* saying that scientific knowledge is free from cultural assumptions, gender biases, metaphysics and such. All they are saying is that it is possible – albeit not always easy – to identify and put these assumptions, biases, etc., to a systematic test of reason and experiment. The danger of *social constructivism and the postmodern theories of science is that they deny that we can ever break out of the prison of our myths, biases and cultural assumptions*: for them, even the best attested knowledge at any time is "local knowledge" of a particular place, time and people. This idea of all science as local science or "ethnoscience" opens the way to indigenist defense of traditions as legitimate sciences. By now there are sufficient number of serious critiques[21] of why social constructivism, including its more politicized feminist epistemology, is based upon faulty reasoning. It is not surprising that Soroush too has written a critique of historicism and postmodernism in science. Unfortunately his philosophical work is not accessible to those who do not know Persian.

A word regarding the politics of knowledge: Sardar and other jet-setting Islamists are feted by Islamic rulers of Saudi Arabia, Pakistan, Malaysia and elsewhere. Our own left wing indigenists – Vandana Shiva, Madhu Kishwar, Claude Alvares, Sundar Lal Bahuguna – are being warmly embraced by neo-Hindu gurus and reactionary publications like *Hinduism Today* and *The Organiser*, the official voice of RSS.[22] Soroush, the Luther of Islam, on the other hand, is facing death-threats and state-sponsored censorship. Before we pat ourselves on the back for Hinduism's tolerance for its rationalists and scientists, let us not forget that Brahmanical Hinduism is replete with strictures against rationalists, skeptics and materialists. Besides, the persecution has already begun: what else does the "retirement" of the left historians mean? If the rest of the India left has got a relatively easy ride so far, it is because the Right finds it easy to co-opt the left-populist anti-globalization, ecological and alternative science and technology campaigns. We hardly have public intellectuals of Soroush's stature and courage who have challenged the worldview of the religious right.

To bring it back to Sarukkai's claims of the incompatibility between the domains of nature and society, science and religion, between doing science and living science, Soroush is obviously denying such incompatibility. (Interestingly, it is the clerical critics of Soroush who, like Sarukkai, are claiming the separation of spheres *fiqh* or faith and science, as two entirely different domains, each with its own separate methodology.) Soroush insists that empirical developments in science have an impact on epistemology: that is, more we learn, the better we can understand how we learn. The new self-understanding of human capabilities can lead to a new understanding of humanity's knowledge of itself, its relationship with nature and human beings' relationship with each other. Like the Enlightenment *philosophes* of the 18th century, Soroush is trying to bring the developments of natural sciences to bear upon how we live with each other, how we reason in society, how we organize our social institutions.

What Sorush is saying is precisely what the doomed idea of "scientific temper" was all about, an idea that was put to a premature end by the Gandhian anti-modernists who used the anti-intellectual philosophies from the West as a "progressive" fig-leaf. In my opinion, the left, including the Marxist left and the secularist-rationalist elements of people's science movements (with honorable exceptions of K.N. Panikkar, K.V. Subbaram and some others), made a momentous mistake in the early 80's by not taking a principled stand in favor of scientific temper as their operating philosophy. Even those who believed in it, began to make public obeisance to traditions, culture and such, or turned their attention purely to economistic critique of development, ignoring the cultural freedoms that are possible with economic development. The populist urge to learn from the wisdom of the unlettered and the oppressed, combined with the fear of the barbed questions of the neo-Gandhians and postmodernists challenging the "*adhikar*" of the supposedly Westernized scientists to commit "epistemic violence" against the innocent traditions of the masses has done untold harm to the cause of secularization of Indian society. We have wasted precious time, and now it is too late.

V. "Things" and "People": Separate Domains?

We are faced with a paradoxical situation. Critics like Sarukkai who see natural science as a social construct deny that knowledge of nature has any relevance for social life. On the other hand, we have Popperians like Soroush, who allow for a relative and progressive *separation* between science and society, who argue that science is relevant for a critique of society. *The more tight the relation between society and science, the less relevance is given to scientific understanding of nature for understanding and/or changing society.* The paradox, of course, is only apparent. Those who tend to read the content and logic of natural science as determined by social interests, will also tend to see any meaning attached to nature as ideological. It follows that they should be more resistant to allowing such reading of nature to influence social behavior. If science is ideology then, allowing scientific understanding to influence society becomes an exercise not of demystification but of ideological naturalization of social power.

Social constructivists deny any analytical distinction between knowledge of nature and structural and cultural morphology of a society. Science, as Sarukkai claims, is simply one mode of "adjudication" through which a society declares some "claims of truth to become 'truth'". The knowledge of nature we acquire through modern science has no special claim to superiority: other cultures have their own socially grounded methods of adjudication among contending claims of truth. On this reading, the "domain of the social" gives meaning to the "domain of nature": nature in itself has no meaning, it is "mute", and "silent" (even though Sarukkai does not refer to it, muteness of nature is a salient idea of the strong program of sociology of science: see the recent writings of Barry Barnes,1992 and David Bloor, 1999, for instance). Different societies give different meanings to nature: some talk of inverse-square gravitational forces, while some talk of *djinns*, but you cannot say that one is an advance over the other. (Sarukkai takes great umbrage at my preference for Newton over the *djinns* and the goddesses of folk sciences. His argument is: "…It is not possible to compare different epistemological systems" and that "different systems of justification embody different norms. And the fight between different systems of knowledge [is]…. about whose norms one should accept." These "norms" of course are seen as above any rational evaluation, as they are historical products embedded in the fabric of a society.)

In social constructivist accounts of science, while the domain of the social is supposed to explain and encompass the domain of nature, the reverse is staunchly denied: that is, *the domain of nature is declared to have no relevance for the domain of the social.* While how we organize our social life is declared to be of primary salience to the meaning we give to nature, *the different meanings we give to nature are deemed to have no relevance for how we organize our social life.* Indeed, any attempt to read social significance in scientific understanding of nature is put down as "reductionist", "scientistic", and worse.

Sarukkai gives expression to this very widespread and deep fear of scientific understanding of nature as somehow turning people into things: "How does an epistemology related to "things" get transformed into an epistemology of social action, unless society and its human constituents are seen as "things.".... Things do not act". On Sarukkai's reading then, replacing a view of nature in which gods keep an account of karma, for instance, with a view of nature that moves by immutable laws which can be understood by all of us, regardless of our karma, makes no difference to how we live and reason together in a society. This is indeed Sarukkai's brief against me, for he repeatedly accuses me of "insufficient understanding" of why the domains of things and people must be kept separate, and why we do not become "caste conscious, or see the evils of sati through cannons of science".

Without any more philosophical hair-splitting, let us look around us and ask if it is indeed true that how Hindu "sciences"– both elite and folk – understand nature has no bearing on the socially regressive, illiberal, anti-human customs we encounter in our everyday life. Let us start with concrete commonplace practices and then peel away the layers of the onion, so to speak, and get to the cosmological views of the "great" traditions of Hinduism that legitimize these practices.

VI. Causes of "Things" and Conquest of Fear

 Let us examine the case of Charanshah who burned herself to death along with her dead husband's body, in November 1999 in Satpura in Bundelkhand, UP. I have no intention of adding to the learned disputations over the "nobility" of this Bharatiya tradition. I am not going to ask whether Charanshah's suicide was or not a sati, and if a sati, how "voluntary" it was. And neither am I about to wallow in the most recent brand of Parisian discourse theory in order to ponder if a subaltern like Charanshah can speak, or whether or not she can act like a "subject" and show "volition" when she throws herself into the flames. Indeed, there is nothing more pathetic than *feminists* looking for signs of female agency and resistance in sati – patriarchy at its most brutal and barbaric. When a woman "chooses" to die because she cannot stomach the idea of lifetime of degradation in widowhood, I don't need any high theory to hear what the subaltern is saying: I can hear, loud and clear, the inhuman traditions that not only make such "choices" possible, but wrap them in an aura of nobility and self-sacrifice.

I am going to leave Charanshah aside and look at the mindset of Charanshah's neighbors and fellow villagers in Satpura and surrounding areas. The media reports are pretty clear about the role of Satpura's residents, Charanshah's neighbors and relatives. It looks like Charanshah was left alone in tending for her husband who was suffering from tuberculosis. The fear was such that, according to *India Today* (Nov. 29, 1999), "the villagers refused to accompany her even to the cremation ground because he had TB". The fact-finding team of All-India Democratic Women's Association reported that the men left the burning pyre unattended while they hurried for a bath, because "the dead man had been a TB patient and they [the mourners] believed that once his body started burning, they might catch infection from it" (*The Hindu*, Dec. 27, 1999). This premature ritual bath has indeed become the community's alibi: they were away bathing and did not know that the widow was heading for a fiery death. *These same villagers who were so reluctant to come to Charanshah's aid when she needed them, and were so perfunctory in whatever assistance they did provide, showed no such compunction when it came to worshipping her as Sati Mata after she was burnt to death.*

Why? Both the act of omission – the villagers' reluctance to help their neighbor in need – and the act of commission – gathering to celebrate their neighbor's horrible self-immolation – need explanation, for both are equally contrary to what one would normally expect from the good and honorable people that the Satpura residents surely are. What led these good men and women to go against the normal standards of morality and neighborly behavior that must surely prevail in their community?

Why did the neighbors not help Charanshah? Why were they in a hurry to cleanse themselves even while the funeral pyre was still hot enough to burn not one but two human bodies (one alive) to ashes? We can rule out caste prejudice. Satpura is a largely dalit village, so it wasn't as if Charanshah was surrounded by some purity-fixated upper castes. Dalits are in fact well known for their culture of mutual help. Why would such people who are free from the irrationality about touchability and purity show such an uncustomary haste for a ritual bath?

They were obviously afraid of catching TB. They evidently thought of TB as a highly contagious disease, which it is not. Such a fear would be rational (because based upon a desire for self-preservation) but false, because it is based upon inadequate and factually wrong understanding of the TB bacillus. Obviously, I have not personally asked the villagers what it was about TB they feared. I am only offering a conjecture that an unscientific, objectively false understanding of the disease influenced Charanshah's community's actions in this matter. Such a conjecture is not entirely far-fetched, for similar fears about leprosy, AIDS and such are quite common in our society.[23]

Sarukkai is right: nature is mute; things don't act, people do. The TB bacilli don't come with labels declaring that they are the ones that cause TB or they will/or won't kill on contact. Indeed, TB bacilli don't reveal themselves to the human eye at all. It is us humans, at least some humans in a particular time and place, who made the bacilli visible under the microscope and connected them to the disease. It is us humans who gave these bacilli the meaning as carriers of a disease. And as we came to understand the behavior of these organisms, we learned better how to avoid them, how to control them, how not to fear them or fear those who have the disease. *How we understand the mute forces of nature influences our sense of ourselves as people and our ethics as neighbors*: Are we subjects of our lives who can exert rational control over our circumstances? Or are we objects on which our circumstances act and all we can do is cringe in fear and hide away when our neighbors need us?

I know that our sophisticated theorists will find my concerns simplistic, hyper-rational and not considerate enough of the people's own knowledge. I will nevertheless persist in my examination for it is these kind of elementary misconceptions, fears and taboos that make up the everyday reality of our society. The point I want to make is simple: human societies are a part of nature, and how we understand nature (both methodologically and substantively) influences how we live with nature and with each other. While nature does not *determine* social behavior, the domain of nature and society are not different "objects of discourse" which cannot be brought in a conversation. Neither are all the different meanings different societies attach to "mute" nature equally good: some meanings, although rational in their own framework of assumptions, are nevertheless objectively false, for they ascribe *wrong* cause and effect relationships between different entities of a phenomenon. Some of these objectively false (even though subjectively meaningful, and even comforting) meanings of nature take a terrible toll on social relations, because they perpetuate fear and hold back full development of human capabilities, which include human kindness, empathy and a sense of commonality. Scientific reason is not an enemy of human goodness as it is made out by the critics. If understood modestly and fallibly, it plays a central role in practical reason in society which includes how people evaluate their options, how they match means to ends, how they plan their lives, in short, how they make moral distinctions.

Indeed, this relationship between objectively correct knowledge and human freedom was amply clear to the ancient Indian materialists who scoffed at the Brahmins' using the fear of death to peddle their doctrines of the immortality of the spirit (Chattopadhyay, 1976, 234). Like their Indian counterparts, the ancient pagans of the classical antiquity of Greece and Rome, were equally aware of the freedom that comes from knowledge. Here is a tribute by Virgil to Titus Lucretius, a poet of the Roman Republic who, like our own Lokayatas, dared to challenge the Platonic idealism of his time:

> Happy the man who can know the causes of things, and has trampled underfoot all fears, inexorable fate and the clamor of greedy hell. (Quoted from Gay, 1966, p. 99).

In their battle against the Christian orthodoxy of their age, the Enlightenment *philosophes* recovered precisely this ancient connection between knowledge of causes and conquest of fear, which as Gay rightly points out, is the "essence of the critical mentality at work". Yes, the Enlightenment *philosophes* turned to their history and their traditions in search for arguments against Christianity. But unlike our romantics, they turned to history to recover the lost voices of the skeptics and the materialists – Lucretius, Cicero, Marcus Aurelius – who they could use as a historical and cultural justification of modern science and humanism. As Peter Gay remarks:

> "[The Enlightenment thinkers] used their classical learning to free themselves from their Christian heritage, and then, having done with the ancients, turned their face toward a modern world view." (p. 8).

The contrast with our own anti-Enlightenment "prophets facing backwards"[24] could not be more stark. Captivated as they are by the siren songs of postmodernity, they have lost confidence in the modern world view. Consequently, when they look back, they retrieve not our Lokayatas, not our ancient skeptics and materialists who insisted upon, at the cost of invoking the wrath of the Brahmanical law-givers, putting the Vedic idealism to the test of experience and logic. No. Our disillusioned anti-modernists look back into Indian traditions and come back with precisely those "wholistic" Brahmanical traditions that have disallowed a separation of the spiritual from the material, and prevented the growth of critical reason in Indian society. All the talk of incommensurability of rationality of East and West will disappear, like mist in the sun, if we were to, like the Enlightenment *philosophes*, recover the suppressed traditions of science and reason that did prevail, despite great odds, among the laboring castes in India's antiquity.

The point of this historical detour into antiquity was simply to remind Indian critics of science of the fundamental connections between knowledge and freedom. Given the deeply entrenched ignorance and unfreedoms that are a part of our cultural heritage, we in India cannot afford to forget or trivialize the liberatory potential of knowledge. This connection has been lost in the unilateral collapse of knowledge into power and ideology of the West. We in India have only worried about the exaggerated power that science has supposedly exerted in the service of colonialism[25] and ignored the deadly power that superstitions and obscurantist ideas have continued to exert on the mental universe of ordinary people. If Indian intellectuals had saved even a fraction of the outrage they express against the "instrumental reason" of modern science and technology, for the palpably real, life-denying, inhuman instrumentalism of our hallowed traditions, we could have made a real and positive difference to the cultural temper of our society, without which no real change is possible.

VII. Dharma as Cosmopolis

But this is hardly the end of the story of Charanshah. We have only examined the act of omission, based upon irrational fear, on part of her community. That was the easy part. I will now look at how a certain view of the natural order, *derived from the core values of Hindu dharma*, goes into the making of the culture of sati. I will argue that while the postmodern critics of science and modernity are anxious to insulate the domain of the social from the domain of nature, *all* religious ideologies base their legitimacy on a putative harmony between their social-ethical prescriptions and the workings of the natural order. By denying that (a) objective scientific knowledge of nature is possible, and (b) that it has any relevance for social ethics, the critics of science disarm any challenge to the religious view of the world. The irony is that these same critics of science continue to count themselves as secularist opponents of Hindutva. I do not doubt their sincerity. But can they oppose the politics of Hindutva consistently and effectively while they *also* oppose the best available means of deconstructing the worldview from which Hindutva gains its intellectual coherence and popular appeal? (Sadly, the tendency to shy away from a critical scrutiny of the actual content of popular Hindu religiosity is common even among the critics of postmodernists who prefer a more "materialist" explanation of the rise of Hindutva.[26] I, on the other hand, believe with Nikki Keddie that new religio-political movements "tend to occur *only* where *in recent decades* religions with strongly supernatural and theistic content are believed in, or strongly identified with, by a large proportion of the population" and where this religiosity is identified with the nation (Keddie, 1998, p. 702, emphasis in the original).[27] A critical engagement with folk religiosity is therefore important.

Let me go back to the issue at hand: namely, the relationship between the domains of "things" and "people", or the relationship between science of nature and society. Let us stay with Charanshah a bit longer. As I did in the last section, I will stay with her relatives and neighbors who saw her death as an event of religious significance. Even granting that the reports of large-scale glorification may have been exaggerated, the fact that the villagers believed that something of great religious significance had happened in Satpura cannot be denied. As long as there are people who continue to treat sati as an act of piety, women will continue to burn.

Whatever else may be in dispute regarding the practice of sati, two facts are beyond doubt. One, that a widow is treated in high Hindu communities as inauspicious; and two, a widow who commits sati is not only not inauspicious but is actually worshipped like a goddess in these same communities. A widow's self-sacrifice is supposed to wash off the inauspiciouness of widowhood.[28]

But what makes a widow inauspicious? And what makes a sati a goddess? The answer to both these questions is to be found in the two central dogmas of Hinduism, namely, karma and *samsara*. Hindu scriptures may or may not explicitly condone widow immolation, but the cosmology which turns a natural event (death) into a moral infraction against women's dharma is enshrined as the very foundation of Hinduism. As Arvind Sharma, an ardent advocate of neo-Hinduism and "Hindu human rights", freely admits, to understand the social significance of sati, one has to understand what is specifically Hindu about it: stripped of what is uniquely Hindu, sati collapses into an ordinary suicide or homicide. Widowhood, according to Sharma, is seen by Hindus as a "karmic crime" of "causing [the]husband's death" and "entails spiritual misfortune and a temporary absence of dharma" (p. 76). Sati is only the most extreme form of yogic austerities (which Sharma calls, appropriately, "*pati-yoga*") that all widows were enjoined to go through in order to "rectify" their lapse from *stri-dharma*: "a sati was viewed …as the very embodiment of the goddess for she expiated *immediately* her bad karma that caused the husband's death. [While] the widow took time to rectify her faults and perfect her yogic discipline to join her husband. The *goal (upeya) was the same for both [the widow and the sati] but the means (upaya) differed.*" (Sharma, 81, emphasis in the original). Thus Sati is only the extreme form of *pati-yoga* which is supposed to bring *punya* to the dead husband, the families and to those who come for *darshan*. This *karmic-yogic* frame explains why a burned-to-death widow is supposed to have miracle-working abilities: yoga, after all, is supposed to develop, among other things, special supernatural powers among the practitioners.[29] This explanation of wife-hood, widowhood and sati is not a purely textual explanation, but is accepted by feminist scholars as the operational ideology of sati (see Chakravarti, 1998 and Narasimhan, 1990). Please note that karma functions here and in Brahmanical Hinduism as a force of nature that transfers actions from the moral realm to the physical realm. The domains of nature and morality are not separate but both obey the same laws of dharma. The karma men and women accumulate by living in obedience with the duties of their dharma translate into their good and bad experienes in their physical lives in here and now. A closer fusion of the domain of nature and moral order would be harder to imagine.

Now, there is enormous amount of sociological, ethnographic, journalistic and everyday, existential data that confirms that the karmic interpretation of widowhood/sati and indeed many other misfortunes ranging from one's caste, illness, childlessness, failure etc. are commonplace in contemporary India. Although as a general rule, the "lower" castes are more immune to, although by no means not entirely free from, karmic interpretations for their "station", there is no denying that the karma doctrine is available, both to the "great" (Sanskritic) and the "little" (popular) traditions of Hinduism, as a "frame of reference that is potentially available in *any* situation that calls for the interpretation of destiny". (Babb, 1983: 171). Contrary to those who read only "resistance" in the subaltern versions of Hinduism, important ethnographic studies (Delige, 1993, Fuller, 1992) show that even when the subaltern seem to create an alternative and a counter-culture for themselves, the terms of this oppositional identity are set by the norms of the Great tradition.

Take for instance, how a middle-aged, Tamil woman, Viramma (whose wonderful first-person account of her life has recently appeared in print) explains her status as a pariah. Her origin story does not invoke the Brahmanical cosmology of Purusha sacrifice and insists upon an original equality of all. Yet, she explains the "lowliness" and "uncleanness" of her caste as but a result from a fall from an earlier situation of equality, as a result of a crime of theft by an ancestor of their caste (Viramma, 1997, p. 165–167) and considers it her dharma to be "humble, obedient, discreet and affectionate". (p. 148). The point is that Viramma ends up reconstructing the Brahmanical idea of impurity and inequality as just deserts for one's own community's actions. Even when she does not use the language of karma or *Purusha*, she accepts – and tries to explain – the "fact" of uncleanness and unworthiness of her caste. The same dynamic becomes apparent in Kancha Ilaiah's *Why I am Not a Hindu*. Despite the strengths of dalit-bahujan culture that

Ilaiah describes so powerfully, it cannot be denied that the ideology of varna and purity still shapes dalit identities: the "mutilation" it inflicts on dalit self-respect ends up as a negative force against which dalit-bahujan have to react, defend and define themselves. One cannot but agree with Christopher Fuller (1992, 256) that the "religion of the oppressed... does not constitute subversive opposition to the social and religious system as a whole. Even when they are resisting elitist pressures to conform, lower social groups consistently tend to reconstruct their own socio-religious inferiority...Inequality is deeply entrenched in Hinduism and Indian society, at both ideological and institutional levels..."

This brief foray into karma doctrine as it plays out in gender and caste relations was meant to establish the continued importance of cultural codes derived from Brahmanical ideology in India's social life, at all strata. This leads me to the issue at hand, namely, the close nexus between the domain of the social and the domain of the natural in Hindu dharma.

I submit to you that Hindu dharma, of which karma is fundamental axiom, maintains its spell on India's cultural ethos because it is *cosmopolis* par excellence. It is a *cosmopolis* in which two of the most inegalitarian ideas of nature – namely, nature as a hierarchical chain of being and nature as an organism – have combined to produce a highly inegalitarian social philosophy. A *cosmopolis* is exactly what it says: it is a cosmos + a polis, a formula that holds that " there is a natural harmony between the order of all the heavens (i.e., the *cosmos*) and the order of human society (i.e., the *polis*) and...[that] human affairs are influenced by, and proceed in step with heavenly affairs..."(Toulmin, 1990: 67).

Although Hinduism is unique in turning the fusion of the natural and the social into a sacred tenet, thinking in terms of a *cosmopolis* is not unique to Hinduism at all. *All* premodern cultures see the society as an organic whole in which natural events have a moral import and, conversely, moral behavior has an effect on the course of nature.[30] The much vaunted "wholism" of non-Western traditions has nothing non-Western about them: they are simply non-modern ways of knowing, which abounded in the West until they were discredited by the combined assault of capitalism, the Reformation, the Scientific Revolution and the Enlightenment. Wholism is simply another name for not separating out what actually belongs to the cosmos, and what belongs to our polis and its traditions myths.

Cosmopolitic thinking serves two important social functions, traces of which continue in modern societies as well. One, by anchoring morality in natural order, it provides human beings with an assurance of permanence and dependability behind the flux of events. In societies where change and innovation are seen as a threat, the belief that there is a permanent order which underwrites people's lives and actions is obviously comforting (Lovin and Reynolds, 1985: 8). Secondly, the view of society as a unified whole with the universe, society as an ordered hierarchy where everyone has his proper place, each place being associated with different rights and duties, obviously serves a legitimating function. What could be more potent as an ideology than making social arrangements as natural, as self-evident, inescapable and necessary as the order in nature itself?

Cosmogony is not unique to Hinduism. But what *is* unique, however, to Sanskritic Hinduism is the view of the natural order and *how* it is mapped on to the social order. Lacking the concept of a law-giver God whose laws of nature make themselves evident in the daily workings of nature which human beings can observe and understand, Hinduism has depended on a monist idealism of the doctrine of Absolute spirit (Brahma) at a Sanskritic level, and on correct ritual and duty at a folk level, as the mediating factor between the *cosmos* and the *polis. In Hinduism, it is not God's natural law that assures a continuity between cosmos and the polis, but dharma.* This dharma does not have an identical content for all: each human group has its own *sva-dharma*, the fulfillment of which maintains the socio-cosmic order.[31]

Why the spell of dharma is so disastrous for the cause of freedom and reason in our society is that it naturalizes hierarchy and hierarchically assigned duties of different varnas and genders. *It makes hierarchy an obligation imposed by the order of nature.* Just as nature has its *rta*, i.e., the universal harmony in which all things in the world have a proper place and function, so do social beings have corresponding places and functions. It does not require much sophisticated discourse analysis to see how dharma anchors social ethics in the alleged order of nature itself. Hindu texts, from learned commentaries of a former President of India, S. Radhakrishnan, to the crude political tracts of the Hindutva brigade, openly acknowledge the inseparability of social ethics and morality from the order of nature. Here is Radhakrishnan (1927, p. 59): "Dharma is virtue in conformity with the *nature of things*; moral evil is disharmony with *the truth which encompasses and controls the world*" (emphasis added). Here is Gandhi who famously declared the 1934 Bihar earthquake to be a "divine chastisement": "Physical phenomena produce results both physical and spiritual. The converse is equally true." Here is Deendayal Upadhyay, the author of *Integral Humanism* that forms the official ideology of the BJP: "When nature is channeled according to the principles of dharma, we have culture and civilization." K.S. Sudarshan (1998), the RSS boss: "All those institutions…and conventions that allow a disturbance free [i.e., harmonious] and untrammeled discourse between an individual, the society, nature and the supreme being, come under the term Dharma."

What is important to understand about the Hindu *cosmopolis* is that the two orders – the natural and the social – do not just mirror each other, but are actually seen as constituting and sustaining each other's functioning. Fulfillment of functions appropriate to the station in life is supposed to be responsible for the maintenance of *rta* (order) in nature, and conversely, improper actions lead to the fall of the universe into unreality, chaos and non-being. *Dharmic actions carry ontological weight.*

Thus, while we moderns and postmoderns may want to deny – for perfectly justifiable reasons, which I as a liberal humanist share – any necessary connection between the working of nature (the realm of necessity) and the social order (the realm of human freedom and choice) , the fact is that the *dominant ideology of Hinduism is premised upon a unity of nature and society*. In the next section, I will elaborate upon why the postmodern-indigenists' embrace of the unity of nature and society as a source of "emancipatory" science is fundamentally misguided and collusive with the Hindu Right. But before I do that, I want to consider the frequently voiced objection that Hindu *shastras* and priests may want to harp upon dharma on the lines described here, but "the people" have somehow escaped the spell of dharma. The "people", it is said, have their own hardy empiricism which allows them to break free from Brahmanical notions of dharma; or that "the people" actually use the dharmic notion of unity of social and the natural to come up with "emancipatory" sciences; or that the dharmic justifications for such crimes against humanity as sati and caste were only given the status of ruling ideology by the colonialists in the first place. These claims come *from the indigenist left*, in the fashionable denunciation of "Orientalism" or "essentialism" and, of any critical examination of the social consequences of Hindu dharma. With "enemies" like these, the Hindu right does not need friends!

Is dharma then only of philosophical interest? And is its effect on the people only benign? Let us see…

a. *Varna*: I have already touched upon the continuing role of karma and varna on dalit consciousness. Here I only want to point out the resurgence of dharma as the official ideology of the Sangh Parivar.

Here is Gandhi – the alleged Mahatma – on *varna-dharma*:
"Varna is not a human invention, but an immutable law of nature...
The law of varna is a special discovery of Hindu seers ...and had
universal application. The world may ignore it today but it will have
to accept it in the time to come" (Gandhi, 1962: 13). I have no use
for the supposed "egalitarianism" of Gandhi and his neo-Hindu,
neo-Vedantist fellow-travelers who have simply declared all varnas
to be equal, by fiat, against all the weight of textual and historical
evidence for a clear hierarchy of values found in the Vedas, Vedanta
and other holy texts of high Hinduism.[32]

And here is one of the true inheritors of Gandhi's conservative
revolution, Deendayal Upadhyay, the inspiration behind the Sangh
Parivar, on why *varna-dharma* is preferable to class struggle: "In our
concept of four castes, they are thought of as analogous to the limbs
of Virat purusha.... [can there] arise any conflict between the head,
the stomach and the legs of the same Purusha? There is a complete
identity of interest, identity of belonging…" If this is not a religious
justification for denying even the possibility of individual autonomy
and plurality of interests, then I don't know what ideology is.

But, one can argue, even the BJP dare not invoke dharma
nowadays to justify caste divisions. Haven't realpolitick interests of
political parties and the rising assertiveness of dalits made dharmic
justifications of caste irrelevant? The answer lies not in words but
in actions. Jan Breman (1999) describes the brutal beating to death
of a halpati in 1994 and suggests that the impunity with which the
dominant castes carried out their crime comes from the injunctions
of Manu they carry in their heads as part of their common sense.
The outrage the upper castes feel at their caste inferiors usurping
their power gets its emotional charge from the righteousness of the
social order in their minds. The victims of *varna dharma* do not
have much use for dharma, even though they inadvertently end
up internalizing some aspects of it (as described earlier). Cosmic/
dharmic understanding of varna has always served as an upper-class,

upper-caste justification for their good karma that earned them a spot among the twice-born. And *that* aspect of dharmic justification of caste is in no danger of disappearing. Far from it! The "social harmony" of *varna dharma* is now a part of the official platform of the BJP, even as it reluctantly gives in to the demands for affirmative action (BJP Election Manifesto, 1998, see also, Jafferlot, 1998). One can hear the echoes of Gandhi and Golwalker's pronouncements on *varna dharma* as a universal law of nature in the more recent advocates of "Hindu science" who present laws of dharma as a product of scientific thinking of our "sages" and in keeping with the most cutting-edge developments of modern ecology and quantum physics (Sudarshan, 1998). Moreover, as Lise McKean has shown in her fine work, as the political and economic salience of Hinduism grows, the much-vaunted values of harmony and cooperation are being sold as a new business ethic to the upwardly mobile classes while at the same time denigrating individual rights as a pathology of the West.

b. *Patriarchy*: I have already touched upon the role of dharma that can transform a death in the family to a case of "karmic crime" of the wife who must atone for it for the rest of her life. But dharmic notion of correspondence between *cosmos* and the *polis*, also serves a more wide-spread and seemingly innocuous – even feminine – function of equating women with nature, earth and the organic. While western xenophiles seeking comforting myths in the spiritual East may find the interconnections between fallow fields and menstruating women most romantic, the fact remains that in actual life, linking of the two serves as a powerful justification for treating women as polluted beings, tied to their menstruating wombs and burdened with obligations to behave as the fecund mother earth. I have dealt exhaustively with the dangerous romance of ecofeminism elsewhere and will not add to it here.

c. *Miracles*, or the instrumental rationality of traditional knowledge: The ontological content of dharma works both ways: it makes human arrangements appear as ordained by nature, and gives the illusion that human interventions can alter the course of nature through supernatural means. Because Hinduism holds divinity to be immanent in nature, the impulse to control nature takes the form not of a study of natural law laid out by a law-giver God, as in Judeo-Christian traditions – much less the fully materialist worldview of modern science – but in propitiating local gods through ritual and prayer. I find it amazing that Indian intellectuals who are so adept at spotting real and imagined depredations of "instrumental reason" of modern science and technology in all its disguises, should be so untroubled by the deadly toll the instrumental reason of traditions takes. Religious rituals are not innocent expressions of simple faith of simple people that are off-limits to critical evaluation by out-of-touch hyper-rational elite. More often than not, religious rituals, yagnas, prayers – even to sacred trees or earth or rivers, much beloved of our ecofeminists – have a component that addresses the very human need to understand and control the forces of nature. Of course, understanding and control of nature is not the sole or the "real" purpose of religion, but it definitely is *one* component – and an important component at that. (Indeed, as Clifford Geertz's classic exposition of "Religion as a Cultural System" suggests, religion gains its hold on the imagination by "clothing [itself] in an aura of facticity".)

In the current left discourse, even among those who have no love lost for the traditional social order, there is a near perfect consensus that any rational critique of popular religious practices is not to be allowed. Such "unadulterated secularism", as Bharucha (1998: 39) calls it, amounts to being "prejudiced" against tradition, seeing it as "fundamentally retrogressive… backward repository of feudal and primitive values". In Bharucha's reading, the progressive writers in an era past, who dared to object to government sponsorship of a *yagna* belonged to this brand of scientific rationalism (p 34). Critics like Nandy, Partha Chatterjee, Dipesh Chakravarty have weighed in with their critique of critical reason as a "derivative discourse" of colonial masters. One wonders what these anti-secular intellectuals will have to say when *yagnas* and prayers become part of official educational and cultural policy, as they are showing all signs of becoming? Yes, they can still object to the mixing of religion and politics on "contingent" or "strategic" grounds – that has always been the last resort of "anti-essentialist" critics of reason. But when political action is divorced from philosophical conviction it soon degenerates into crass opportunism.

Let me take a couple of contemporary examples and ask how our critics of secular-rationalists would respond. I will go back to Viramma, whose honest, down-to-earth account of her trials, tribulations and triumphs I find most touching. She is a woman who can combine faith in gods with a great deal of common sense. The gods she worships are non-Sanskritic gods and goddesses of her paraiayar caste, although she surreptitiously listens in – from a respectful distance – to the religious ceremonies of the upper castes. Her relationship with her own gods is most intimate: she sings to them, offers animal sacrifices to them and goes to pilgrimages, the expense for which she can barely afford. But it is amply clear that her faith is not devoid of instrumental reason: her piety is *also* a means to an end of warding off evil spirits and illnesses. At one occasion that captures the complex dynamic of faith, caste ideology and instrumental reason, Viramma ascribes the temporary loss of her milk (she is nursing her baby) to her "crime" of having listened in to the prayers to upper-caste, superior gods in her master's house. Her "unclean-ness," she believes, has brought upon her the wrath of the goddess. I cannot find a more telling example of the ideological work of religious faith. No doubt that Viramma's religiosity is very earthy, practical and egalitarian – pretty much as described by Ilaiah. But Viramma accepts her gods as inferior to the gods of the clean castes. Moreover – and here I have a problem with Ilaiah's celebratory view of dalit religiosity – her faith in the protective powers of gods did nothing to save nine of her twelve children from dying of perfectly curable infectious diseases. If dalits are to serve as the agents of reason and Enlightenment in Indian society, they will have to accept that reason will expel their own gods, as well as the gods of the twice-borns, from social life.

Any misconception that such instrumental uses of religious faith is only limited to poor people and will go away as more modern alternatives become available, ought to disappear on reading Lise McKean's account of well-heeled, urban middle-to-upper-class devotees of modern gurus who run modern, profit-making, technologically sophisticated ashrams (not unlike the rich fundamentalist outfits in the US). (Most of these gurus are ardent supporters of VHP and the rest of the Sangh Parivar). It is clear that faith in the miracle-working powers of gurus feeds upon the dharmic notions of *karma*, *yoga* and *moksha*: the gurus, through their asceticism have accumulated sufficient power, that they can alter the course of nature which – recall from our earlier discussion of cosmopolis – follows the same course as dutiful, righteous action.

The point I am trying to make is this: the religiosity of people is not just a matter of simple faith – the supposed antithesis of the derided "instrumental reason" of modern science and technology. And neither is this religiosity simply an ideological cover for "real" material needs. This religiosity has roots in the actual doctrines and worldview of Hindu dharma which sanction an irrational route to solving the problems of here and now.

I agree that religious sentiments cannot be reduced without a residue *only* to stand-ins for cognition and control. But there is no need to over-correct the reductionism of rationalists and swing to the other extreme and ignore the cognitive-instrumental needs religious beliefs *do* actually serve. In fact, one must take Geertz's understanding of religion seriously and consider the possibility that religious beliefs masquerade as facts of nature in order to gain acceptability. If "man" does not live by reason alone, he does not live by faith alone either: faith can use reason as its vehicle to lodge itself in human consciousness. In fact, in order to protect true faith – which does not need subterfuge of reason – it is important to tease out the two components of religious beliefs. That is the reason that, unlike our basically secular and non-believing defenders of "the people's" faith and traditions, those internal critics of religion who are men and women of faith (e.g., Soroush in Iran, and any number of modernist priests and theologians in the West), have not hesitated in exposing inherited religious beliefs to critical reason: they did that more out of a desire to put faith on a secure ground than to spread rationalist skepticism all around. In India, as even the most ardent neo-Hindus readily grant, the impulse to reform religion from within has been very weak and has invariably fallen prey to the Brahmanical-nationalist interest in absorbing heterodoxies into the supposedly universal core of Hinduism. Out of necessity, the task of religious reform has fallen to lay intellectuals. Apart from a small but principled minority, Indian intellectuals have not taken on a critique of religious reason with the seriousness it deserves.

VIII. Breaking the Cosmopolis: The Historical Role of Reason

Life in a *cosmopolis* is stifling: man-made laws are backed by the alleged force of nature, and the keepers of these laws – the god-men, the gurus and the priests – correspondingly acquire an aura of unquestioned authority in both the sacred and the secular realms. Justifiably, we moderns (and postmoderns) are vehemently opposed to any natural – or supernatural – justifications for man-made laws. (This explains Sarukkai's mocking condescension toward my argument that the cultural universe we live in India today stands to be liberated if what we know about nature through science is allowed to challenge what our dharmic sources tell us about the world. To a postmodernist like Sarukkai, it is simply unimaginable and morally abhorrent that any aspect of nature can or should illuminate social ethic.) It is this fundamentally sound distaste for *cosmopolis* – which

I as a liberal humanist share – that underlies the postmodern rebellion against modern science. The critics of science fear that modern science's claim to have discovered objective truths of nature will legitimize attempts to restore *cosmopolis* in a modern disguise, i.e., to justify the capitalist social order as ordained by nature.

What I find objectionable about postmodernist-indigenist attacks on science is not their distaste for *cosmopolis*, but their misguided and distorted understanding of modern science as an ideology of *cosmopolis*. What I object to, in other words, is the completely a-historical and factually incorrect understanding of modern science as a discourse that justifies the interest of the powerful by making their power look natural. While *science as an instrument* has sometimes served the interest of power, science *as a worldview* has been the solvent of the *cosmopolis*. Indeed, the historical record clearly shows, despite all the blind-alleys of scientific racism, breaking down the premodern *cosmopolis* has been the crowning achievement of modern science. Consequently, I will argue, it is simply inconsistent, philosophically, on the part of postmodernist-indigenists to simultaneously want to end any naturalistic justifications for social arrangements *and* to deny the possibility of rational progress in modern science. These critics are trying to get the world that the Enlightenment made – i.e., a world where the *cosmos* and the *polis* are not expected to march in lock step – without the protracted and personally painful struggle against one's own inheritance that the Enlightenment calls for. The postcolonial intellectuals' embrace of postmodernist concerns and postmodernist frames of thought, without first becoming modern, is a replay in the realm of culture of the communist left's hurry to get to the ultimate bliss of a classless society without a bourgeois revolution.[33] Both, I contend, are routes to the same unintended end of reactionary modernism, with postmodernism being the ideology of reactionary modernism of the right. Reactionary modernism, either of the right or of the left, can promise highly sophisticated modern technology, without the benefit of political liberalism in the public sphere. India – with nuclear bombs in the silos and "Vedic science" in the schools – is showing all the signs of a dangerous reconciliation between forces of modernity and atavistic social philosophies. Such a reconciliation has been tried once before – in Nazi Germany (Herf, 1984).

I submit that two of the most fundamental concessions to Hindutva's reactionary modernism that the postmodernist-indigenist critics of modern science have made are: a.) That "we" the oppressed/colonized/East think "wholistically", while "they" the oppressors/colonizers/West think "reductionistically", and b.) that thinking holistically will lead to "emancipatory" science. This supposed wholist, non-dualistic, non-reductionist standpoint epistemology of the oppressed, is precisely the philosophy of "integral humanism" so dear to Hindutvawadis. The much vaunted "non-dualism" of Vedanta that is the foundation of all neo-Hindu revivalists from Vivekanand onward, is nothing but the religious right's version of the postmodernist left's agitation on behalf of the supposedly incommensurate differences in the criteria of validity of experience, reason and truth between the West/colonizers/men and the East/the colonized/women.

The fact is that both *"wholistic"*[34] *and "reductionist"*[35] *thinking are historical modes of thought*: the pre-capitalist West was no less "wholist" than the East. What is more, transition from wholist to "reductionist" thinking is not the disaster that it is made out to be. "Reductionism" is nothing but a cognitive – and concomitantly, a political – ethic that demands of its practitioners to make all honest effort to separate the influence of the polis when they study the *cosmos* and vice versa. *It is an ethic that demands that we take apart the package deal between nature and society that our priests, our gurus, our traditions offer us, and analyze the two in terms that we, ordinary mortals, can ascertain through our own reason and senses.* Reductionism is an ethic based upon Kant's insistence to seek guarantee of our social morality not in nature, or in God, or in any external source of authority – and that includes the party, the proletariat, women, "people of color" or any group that can claim an "epistemological privilege" based upon either their power or their lack of it – but in the "categorical apparatus" of our own minds and reason, disciplined by a collective, and free exercise of reason by all in public life. (Lest this account of the historical role of reason be put aside as "positivist", it is significant to point out that such staunch social-democratic critics of positivism as Jurgen Habermas, Hilary Putnam, Richard Bernstein, Seyla Benhabib subscribe to this communicative ethic over a special epistemic privilege of the oppressed.)[36]

It is this much ridiculed "reductionism", or "dualism" between object (nature) and subject (the culturally shaped mind) that, slowly but surely, drove the gods out of the cosmos (though not necessarily out of the life in the *polis* – gods could stay in the *polis* as objects of personal faith, but not as final causes of natural events). It is the scientific refusal to recognize any source of epistemic privilege that translates, in society, into a refusal to bow to anyone. Nothing and no-one is sacred but a *procedure* in which potentially any one, with due education and training can participate. No doubt this ethic is nowhere fully and perfectly realized – and perhaps should never, even in principle, be fully realized, for men and women do not live by procedural reason alone. Moreover, those seeking a socialist society find the new culture of reason complicit in the bourgeois order, for it upholds formal and procedural equality of individuals without challenging the class privileges of the bourgeoisie. For all the admitted limitations, both inherent and contingent, reason still remains a force for permanent revolution in a society. Those of us who aspire for a liberal, democratic socialism in which no one can rule on the behalf of all, in which there is no fount of liberatory consciousness, cannot afford to deny the very possibility of critical reason, as postmodernists and social constructivists do.

I know that postmodernists and their sympathizers will assert most strenuously that they are not denying reason, but only challenging its claims to universalism and cognitive superiority over other ways of knowing. By now, all the standard postmodern arguments have been repeated ad nauseum. Sarukkai repeats the tired old cliches: scientific justification is only one variant of how "claims of truth become truth" (Sarukkai, p. 779); other cultures use their own norms for justifying *their* claims of truth (783); modern science establishes its Western norms of justification by "forced exclusion" of other rationalities (p. 781), which are presumably as capable of "adjudication" of truth claims, etc. In my previous writings, I have challenged the philosophical grounds for theories of "alternative epistemologies", which Sarukkai espouses. Rather than repeat myself, I want to extend a challenge to Sarukkai. Will he please tell us, how he will respond to the votaries of Hindu science who claim – in almost the exact tone and vocabulary that Saruakkai uses to decry the exclusiveness of modern science – that karma is an exact science, at par with the discovery of laws of gravity by Newton, for it can predict and explain events in human and natural life (see Sundarshan, for example, although the claim is present in such sophisticated neo-Hindus as Radhakrishnan as well)? Here is one cultural tradition "adjudicating" and proclaiming the truth of culturally sanctioned experiences of nature and society. Would Sarukkai grant that this adjudication is at par with science? If not, why not?

Those of us who are concerned with the rise of state-backed revivalism have no choice but to rethink the deference to traditions we ourselves have shown. This rethinking need not take us back to positivism – for cultural discourse and traditions do indeed guide our empirical experiences and our reasons. But we need to recover a respect for critical reason that remains committed to the belief that we can become aware of our prejudices and learn to evaluate them rationally through free, open and critical debates.

IX. Conclusion

In one of his last important books, *Postmodernism, Reason and Religion*, Ernest Gellner described three major contestants in the global intellectual conflict at the close of the millennium: religious fundamentalism, relativism/postmodernism and Enlightenment rationalism, or what Gellner jokingly calls "rationalist fundamentalism".

Like Gellner, I am a proud and unrepentant adherent of Enlightenment rationalism. This essay was meant as a call for reviving the prematurely aborted project of Enlightenment in India. The indigenist intellectual dalliance with postmodernism has only aided the rise of reactionary modernism of Hindutva. Even though the religious right has no use for the deeply anti-essentialist and secularizing possibilities of postmodern thought, postmodernist denigration of reason has provided the grounds for the revivalist project of Hindu science and Hindu modernity. Enlightenment rationalism is the only viable, long-term solution to the crisis that India faces today.

Notes

1   This paper first appeared in *Economic and Political Weekly*, July 7, 2001.

2   There are those avowed anti-secularists who have argued that nothing has changed, that *Hindutvawadis* are only more open, less hypocritical variants of Nehruvian "pseudo-secularists", for they both seek the same goal of modern "unmarked" culturally-denuded "abstract individuals", (see Nivedita Menon's (1998) twist on Nandy's well known argument) and that the whole idea of keeping religiosity out of the public realm is wrong-headed and unsuited to Indian culture in the first place. But these well-known anti-secularists apart, there is a general feeling among those who oppose the Sangh parivar that the Nehruvian secularism mostly meant a formal nod to secular ideas, with very little principled commitment to them.

There is a substance to these concerns. As I will argue here, the battle for secularism and humanism was never joined at the terrain of culture; the secularists – and here not just the Nehruvian liberals but all other left intellectuals share the blame – never adequately challenged the pervasive and reactionary influence of religious thought on the hearts and minds of Indians.

Nevertheless, it is facile to deny any difference between the Nehruvian secularism and what has now come to pass. There is an essential difference: while the communalism of the former, deplorable as it was, was a matter of unprincipled political opportunism, that of the latter is grounded in the ideals of *dharma rajya*. There is no conflict between the ideals and the actual practice in the case of BJP. Sometimes, even lip-service to formal principles has its uses, for it provides a vantage point from where to hold the state accountable for delivering on the formal principles.

3   This does not mean that I do not recognize the pervasive influence of the power of money and privilege in Western societies. But the proposition that social institutions in western democracies do not humiliate their citizens on an everyday basis can be supported by a comparative study of institutions across cultures and political systems. Instances of humiliation – like Rodney King's beating by Los Angeles police – make news around the world precisely because they are relatively rare and because they contradict the well-established norms of fairness and justice.

4   Needless to say, the natural equality of all is still not fully realized in even the most advanced countries. Social inequities have to be recognized but should not be allowed to trivialize, as they often are in "radical" discourse, the importance of the recognition of the *principle* of the equality of natural reason. Such a principle is not at all self-evident, even to this date, in Brahmanical Hinduism.

5   It was this spirit of intellectual modesty and anti-dogmatism that constituted the self-understanding of the Enlightenment and *not* the delusions of grandeur contemporary critics have read into them. This understanding is based upon not just the earlier, more sympathetic commentators like Peter Gay (1969) and Ernest Cassirer (1951), but also contemporary students of Enlightenment who read it through their encounter with postmodernism. Notable among the latter are: Porter (1992), Outram (1995), Bronner (1995), Dranton (1997) and Gordon (1999).

6   Jurgen Habermas (see Calhoun, 1997) remains the best source for a history of the structural transformation of the public sphere.

7   In *The Jewish Question*, Marx made it plain that he saw the rights of man of the American and of the French declarations as "nothing but the rights of members of civil society, i.e., the rights of egotistic man, of man separated

from other men and from the community". Recognition of such rights by modern state, in his opinion, "has no other meaning than the recognition of slavery by the state of antiquity had".

Yet, it cannot be denied that Marx himself and Marxist social movements have led the struggle for securing human and civil rights around the world.

8   While the Protestant Reformation did indeed purge the medieval church of miracles and superstitions, it actually led to an increase in magic, witchcraft and other supernatural beliefs in the rest of the society, primarily because the Catholic church was no longer available to minister to those material and emotional needs that miracles and supernatural beliefs answered. The classic text that examines the influence of Reformation on popular beliefs is Keith Thomas (1971) .

9   The Scientific Revolution did not mark a break with the Christian world view. All the major figures of the Scientific Revolution continued to be pious Christians.

10   Although capitalist social relations do have a tendency to "melt all that is solid", they can also selectively conserve the magical and mystical beliefs that serve the profit-motive. The use of ideologies of karma and bhakti by Indian industrialists has been studied by Milton Singer (1972). Lise McKeane (1998) offers new evidence of the accommodative tendencies of Hinduism. She describes neo-Hindu gurus who are modernizing elements of Hindu worldview to serve as ideology of the new, globalized business classes. Indeed, the ability of Indian traditions to accommodate modern capitalist development is what the whole thesis of "modernity of traditions" is all about.

11   Many streams of "progressive" thought have converged to shape this post-Enlightenment common sense. Most persistent and far-reaching critiques of reason have come from feminists (notably, Sandra Harding, Helen Longino, Evelyn Fox Keller, Donna Haraway, Vandana Shiva) and the proponents of "alternative sciences" (notably, Ashis Nandy and the so-called "Delhi School", Ziauddin Sardar and the allied proponents of the so-called "Islamic science".) This style of science critique finds philosophical justification from a radicalized Kuhnian sociology of science on the one hand, and the Foucaultian critiques of Orientalism on the other. As most of these works have become contemporary classics, complete references are not included in this paper.

12   See Saberwal, 1995 for the segmentary logic of caste, and see S. Gopal, 1996, Upadhyay, 1992 and Larson, 1995 for the continued influence of neo-Hindu ideology on India's brand of secularism.

13   See Gurpreet Mahajan's (1995) critique of this tendency. .

14 Javeed Alam (1999) is a good example of common Marxist misconceptions about the politics and epistemology of the Enlightenment.

15 Hindutva right wants to keep the economic freedoms of the market, while denying as un-Hindu the individual freedoms and rights of liberalism.

16 This is not to deny that the dalit–OBC politics has its share of opportunism, identity politics and sheer chauvinism. But the philosophical underpinnings of dalit-OBC movements are derived, most consistently, from the Enlightenment view of the world.

17 Gerald Larson (1995) provides a very sympathetic reading of how neo-Hinduism has provided the political philosophy of post-colonial India.

18 While there always had been some isolated dissidents, the first major critique of constructivism appeared in 1994 with the publication of *Higher Superstition: The Academic Left and its Quarrel with Science* by Paul Gross, a molecular biologist and Norman Levitt, a mathematician. The book was followed with a conference organized by the New York Academy of Sciences. The proceedings of this conference were published in a volume titled *Flight From Reason and Science*. In the interest of full disclosure, I must mention that one of my essays appears in the Flight volume.

19 For a recent compendium of writings of anti-constructivist philosophers of science, see Koertge (1998).

20 To anticipate the usual complaints: Yes, it is possible to deify science itself as a new religion. But no, it does not mean that science by its nature is a new myth. It only means that we need a constant vigilance against all mythic thinking. The dialectic of Enlightenment can only be cured by a more radicalized Enlightenment.

21 Including my own Nanda, 1997, but also see Koertge, 1998, Kitcher, Laudan, and Haack, and the original works of Karl Popper and the American pragmatists, especially Charles S. Peirce and John Dewey.

22 On nearly any issue pertaining to women from domestic violence to quotas for women, *Hinduism Today* runs special interviews with Madhu Kishwar, or reprints her writings. On matters of ecology, globalization, intellectual property, *The Organiser* turns to Vandana Shiva. Hindutva writings on relevance of Hinduism to ecological preservation are replete with the Shiva's and occasionally, Patkar's invocation of nature as mother, shakti and such. Claude Alvares' writings get kudos among the Hindutva critics of modernity. Lise McKean (p. 261) reports the appearance and the stirring speech by Sundarlal Bahuguna of the Chipko fame in the praise of Bharatiya Sanskriti to combat the evils of science and modernity at the centenary celebrations of Sivananda's Divine Life Society in Haridwar. The

founding guru of Divine Life Society was one of the founding members of VHP.

23 This is not to suggest that the West is entirely free from irrationalities. Fear of those with AIDS is widespread in the US. It is not an all-or-nothing issue, but more of a continuum. India has to go longer on the continuum to become a more rational society.

24 *Prophets Facing Backwards: Postmodernism, Science, and Hindu Nationalism* is the title of my new book which examines the philosophical fallacies of postmodern critiques of science and their hold on Indian "alternative science movements".

25 How little colonialism or even postcolonial modernity actually changed the basic tenor of Hindu worldview is well described in Gerald Larson (1995), whose defense of neo-Hinduism inadvertently reveals the continuities that have withstood and absorbed the colonial ideas within Hinduism. Indeed, even a cursory reading of Radhakrishnan reveals how deeply entrenched the architects of modern India were in a Brahmanical worldview, complete with its justifications for caste and patriarchy.

26 Here I have my good friend Achin Vanaik in mind, from whose otherwise excellent writings I have learned so much.

27 The fact that mass religiosity of a strongly super-naturalistic kind is a contributory factor in the rise of religious politics makes the anti-Enlightenment bias of the Indian Left all the more distressing. The populist turn to traditional values has only ended up deifying as "decolonization of the mind" what needed to be questioned. Decolonization to what end? Whether intended or not, the mental decolonization has only prepared the great hope of the Indian left – the "people", the "subaltern" – for a take-over by the Hindu Right. This nexus between "critical traditionalism" and neo-Hinduism has been visible for all to see since Gandhi and later the JP movement. It appears to me that Indian left intellectuals must first break the spell of dharma from their own minds before they can approach the cultural question with any degree of balance.

28 Unless this worldview changes, we cannot hope to alter the status of widows. Calls for more development etc. as the answer to Satpura tragedy are perfectly legitimate. But it is not clear at all if material development by itself translates into a modernization of consciousness. On the contrary, there is ample evidence to suggest that the habits of the heart, conditioned by a host of intimate social relations and institutions, can bend the changing modes of production to their own continued survival.

29 Interestingly, at the end of his phenomenological analysis of what is specifically Hindu about sati, Sharma seems to have one great regret: these poor widows and satis were not told, and neither were they perceived by

others, as actually doing yoga . If *pati-yoga* could be seen as a form of yoga rather than just plain old drudgery, widows could get the respect that is due to a yogic! So, keep widowhood, only call it yoga! (Although to be fair to Sharma, he does come down against Sati on the ground that unlike real yogis, women do not choose the yogic path as their vocation).

30 See Gellner, 1992, Popper 1962 for classic statements of the history of reason in society. Patricia Crone (1989) provides a useful introduction.

31 If a theoretical statement of this idea of (*sva*)-dharma, which is familiar to anyone – non-Hindus included – growing up in India is needed at all, see Biardeau, 1989.

32 For a clear, textually grounded, learned – and without any over-heated rhetoric – analysis of the support of hierarchy in the Vedas and Vedanta, see the writings of Wilhelm Halbfass (1988, 1991).

33 This does not imply that I subscribe to universal laws of history. Neither a bourgeois revolution in social relations nor a class-less society is inevitable. But they become possible to imagine, for the first time in history, with the forces unleashed by science, industry and capitalism.

34 Technically, the term "holism" describes any doctrine that emphasizes the priority of a whole over its parts. In discourse theory, holism claims that the meaning of an individual word can only be understood in terms of its relation to an indefinitely larger body of language, such as a whole theory, or even a whole language or form of life. (Blackburn, 1994). In multicultural and postcolonial critiques, holism comes to take connotations of unity, or lack of separation of knowledge and culture, facts and values.

35 Technically, the term "reductionism" holds that the "facts or entities apparently needed to make true the statements of some area of discourse are dispensable in favor of some other facts or entities" (Blackburn, 1994). Thus one might advocate reducing biology to chemistry, or chemistry to physics. Reductionism assumes a unity of science so that laws of any special branch of science can be described as special cases of the universal way things are.

However, multicultural and postcolonial critics of science use reductionism more in its historical sense of differentiation between the spheres of factual knowledge and sphere of philosophy, theology and ethics (See Gellner, 1992). Reductionism here comes to take on a connotation of separation of knowledge from culture, facts from values.

36 My own account here is indebted to Karl Popper (1962) and Ernest Gellner (1992). For an earlier statement of this historical role of reason for postcolonial societies, see Nanda (1996).

References

Alam, Javeed. 1999. *India: Living with Modernity*. New Delhi: Oxford.

Babb, Lawrence. Destiny and Responsibility: Karma in Popular Hinduism. In Charles Keyes and Valentine Daniel (eds.), *Karma: An Anthropological Inquiry*. Berkeley: University of Chicago Press.

Barnes, Barry. 1992. Realism, Relativism and Finitism. In Raven, D. et al., (eds.) *Cognitive Relativism and Social Sciences*. New Bruswick: Transaction.

Barnes, Barry and David Bloor. 1982. Relativism, Rationalism and Sociology of Knowledge. In Martin Hollis and Steven Lukes (eds.), *Rationality and Relativism*. MIT Press.

Bharucha, Rustom. 1998. *In the Name of the Secular: Contemporary Cultural Activism in India*. Oxford.

Biardeau, Madeline. 1989. *Hinduism: The Anthropology of a Civilization*. Oxford University Press.

Blackburn, Simon. 1994. *The Oxford Dictionary of Philosophy*. New York, Oxford University Press.

Bloor, David 1999. *Anti-Latour. Studies in History and Philosophy of Science*. Vol. 30 (1): 81–112.

Breman, Jan. 1999. Silencing the Voice of Agricultural Laborers in South Gujarat. *Modern Asian Studies*, 33.

Bronner, Stephen. 1995. The Enlightenment and its Critics. *New Politics*. Spring, 65–86.

Calhoun, Craig. 1997. *Habermas and the Public Sphere*. MIT Press.

Cassierer, Ernest. 1951. *The Philosophy of the Enlightenment*. Princeton University Press.

Chakrabarty, Dipesh. 1995. Radical Histories and Question of Enlightenment Rationalism. *Economic and Political Weekly*, April 8.

Chakravarti, Uma, 1993. Conceptualizing Brahmanical Patriarchy in Early India: Gender, Caste, Class and State. *Economic and Political Weekly*, April 3: 579–585.

——. 1998. Gender, Caste and Labor: The Ideological and Material Structure of Widowhood. In Martha A. Chen (ed.) *Widows in India: Social Neglect and Public Action*. New Delhi: Sage

Chattopadhyay, Debiprasad. 1976. *What is Living and What is Dead in Indian Philosophy*. New Delhi: People's Publishing House.

Crone, Patricia. 1989. *Pre-Industrial Societies*. Blackwell.

Darnton, Robert. 1997. George Washington's False Teeth. *New York Review of Books*. March 27.

Feuerstein, Georg, Subhash Kak and David Frawley. 1995. *In Search for the Cradle of Civilization: New Light on Ancient India*. Illinois: Quest Books.

Fuller, C.J. 1992. *The Camphor Flame: Popular Hinduism and Society in India*. Princeton University Press.

Gandhi, M.K. 1962. *Varnashramdharma*. Navjivan Publishing House.

Gordon, Daniel. 1999. The Supposed Obsolescence of the French Enlightenment. *Historical Reflections*. Vol. 25 (2): 365–385.

Gross, Paul and Norman Levitt. 1994. *Higher Superstition: The Academic Left and its Quarrel with Science* (Johns Hopkins Press)

Gross, Paul, Norman Levitt and Martin Lewis. 1996. *The Flight From Reason and Science*. New York Academy of Sciences.

Gay, Peter. 1959. *The Party of Humanity*. NY: Norton.

——. 1966. *The Enlightenment: An Interpretation*. Vol. 1: *The Rise of Modern Paganism*. NY: Norton.

——. 1966. *The Enlightenment: An interpretation*. Vol.2: *The Science of Freedom*. NY: Norton

Gellner, Ernest. 1992. *Reason and Culture*. Blackwell.

Gopal. S. 1996. Nehru, Religion and Secularism. In R. Champalakshami and S. Gopal (eds.) *Tradition, Dissent and Ideology: Essays in Honor of Romila Thapar*. New Delhi: Oxford University Press.

Halbfass, Wilhelm. 1988. *India and Europe: An Essay in Understanding*. Albany: SUNY Press.

——. 1991. *Tradition and Reflection: Explorations in Indian Thought*. Albany: SUNY Press.

Hamspson, Norman. *The French Revolution.*

Herf, Jeffrey. 1984. *Reactionary Modernism: Technology, Culture and Politics in Weimar and the Third Reich.* Cambridge University Press.

Human Development Report, 1996. New York: Oxford University Press.

Jafferlot, Christophe (1998).BJP and the Caste Barrier: Beyond the Twice-born? In Thomas B. Hansen and Christophe Jafferlot (eds.) *The BJP and the Compulsion of Politics in India.* New Delhi: Oxford.

Jodha, N.S. 1988. Poverty Debate in India: A Minority View. *Economic and Political Weekly*, Special Issue, Nov.

Kakar, Sudhir. 1981. *The Inner World.* New Delhi: Oxford University Press.

Keddie, Nikki. 1998. The New Religious Politics: Where, When and Why do "Fundamentalisms" Appear? *Comparative Studies of Society and History.*

Koertge, Noretta (ed.) 1998. *A House Built On Sand: Exposing Postmodern Myths about Science.* NY: Oxford University Press.

Larson, Gerald. 1995. *India's Agony Over Religion.* Albany: SUNY Press.

Lovin, Robin and Frank Reynolds. 1985. *Cosmogony and Ethical Order: New Studies in Comparative Ethics.* University of Chicago Press.

Mahajan, Gurpreet. 1995. Cultural Embodiment and Histories: Towards Construction of Self. In Upendra Baxi and Bhikhu Parekh (eds.), *Crisis and Change in Contemporary India.* New Delhi: Sage.

Mahoney, William. Hindu Dharma. *Encyclopedia of Religion.*

McKean, Lise. 1996. *Divine Enterprise: Gurus and the Hindu Nationalist Movement.* Chicago: Chicago University Press.

Menon, Nivedita. 1998. State/Gender/ Community: Citizenship in Contemporary India. *Economic and Political Weekly.* Jan 31: PE3–PE 10.

Nanda, Meera. 1996. The Science Question in Postcolonial Feminism. In Gross, Levitt and Lewis (eds.), op. cit.

——. 1998. Epistemic Charity of Social Constructivist Theories of Science and Why the Third World Must Reject the Offer. In Koertege.(ed), op. cit.

Nandy, Ashish. 1983. *The Intimate Enemy*. Oxford University Press.

Narasimhan, Sakuntala. 1990. *Sati: Widow Burning in India*. New York: Doubleday.

Omvedt, Gail.1994.*Dalits and the Democratic Revolution: Dr. Ambedkar and the Dalit Movement in Colonial India*. New Delhi: Sage.

Outram, Dorinda. 1995. *The Enlightenment*. Cambridge University Press.

Popper, Karl. 1962. *Open Society and Its Enemies*. Vol. 1 and 2. Princeton University Press.

Porter, Roy. 1992. *The Enlightenment*. McMillan.

Radhakrishnan, S. 1927. *Hindu View of Life*. Harper Collins (India).

Sen, Amartya. 2000. East and West: The Reach of Reason. *New York Review of Books*, July 20.

Sharma, Arvind. 1988. *Sati: Historical and Phenomenological Essays*. New Delhi: Motilal Banarsidas.

Singer, Milton. 1972. *When A Great Tradition Modernizes*. Chicago University Press.

Sokal, Alan and Jean Bricmont. 1998. *Fashionable Nonsense: Postmodern Intellecutals' Abuse of Science*. New York: Picador.

Soroush, Abdol Karim, The Evolution and Devolution of Religious Knowledge. In Charles Kurzman (ed.) *Liberal Islam: A Sourcebook*. NY: Oxford University Press. 1998.

Sudarshan, K.S. 1998. Hindu Dharma and its Scientific Spirit. *Prajna Journal*, Vol 2, No. 2 .

Thomas, Keith. 1971. *Religion and the Decline of Magic*. New York: Scribner.

Toulmin, Stephen. 1990. *Cosmopolis: the Hidden Agenda of Modernity*. Chicago University Press.

Upadhyaya, Deendayal. 1965. *Integral Humanism*. (http://www.Hindu.org/)

Upadhyaya, Prakash C. 1992. The Politics of Indian Secularism. *Modern Asian Studies*, 26(4): 815–853.

Viramma, Josiane and Jean Luc Racine. 1997. *Viramma: Life of an Untouchable*. London: Verso, and Paris: UNESCO.

How Modern Are We?
Cultural Contradictions of India's Modernity*

Berlin, 1783. A debating club called 'Berliner Mittwocchgesellschaft' (the Berlin Wednesday Club) invited its members to respond to this question: "What is Enlightenment?" A strenuous debate followed. The philosopher Immanuel Kant joined in the fray with his well known essay, 'Answer to the Question: What Is Enlightenment?' This is how Kant characterised what was distinctive about the ferment of ideas sweeping 18th century Europe:

> Enlightenment is man's release from this self-incurred immaturity [which is] his inability to make use of his understanding without direction from another…*Sapere aude*! "Have courage to use your own reason!" that is the motto of the enlightenment.

I

The reader might justifiably wonder why an essay about India in the 21st century should begin with what Immanuel Kant wrote back in the 18th century. What possible relevance can these musty old European debates have for India today?

I believe that the transformation of reason brought about by the scientific revolution that so impressed Kant and other

Enlightenment thinkers holds the key to the fulfilment of the programme of disenchantment and secularisation everywhere. Kant's call of '*Sapere aude!*' was simultaneously an invocation of a new standard of reason meant to challenge all *a priori* truths that we accept out of faith, cultural conditioning or overt indoctrination. Once we understand the transformation of reason that the scientific revolution and the Enlightenment set in motion, we will be in a better position to understand why modernity in India has this feel of incompleteness, superficiality and even schizophrenia.

Modern India has embraced the end products of the scientific revolution and the Enlightenment in the west namely, modern technology and a liberal-secular framework of laws encoded in the Constitution. But it has done so without challenging the cultural authority of the supernatural and mystical world view derived from the idealistic strands of Hinduism. If anything, from its very beginning in the Bengal renaissance, India's project of modernity has evolved within a uniquely Indian inclusive style of counter-Enlightenment. By counter-Enlightenment I mean only this: in a stark contrast to the Enlightenment project of bringing religion within the limits of scientific reason, the Indian counter-Enlightenment has tended to subsume or co-opt scientific reason within the spirit-based cosmology and epistemology of "the Vedas".[1] Since independence, India has created an impressive workforce of scientists and engineers, many of them doing fairly advanced science which meets the standards of excellence in the best laboratories in the rest of the world. But India's science has not evolved out of a critical engagement with the religious commonsense that still pervades the cultural life outside and often inside the labs. Modern ideas and innovations are being incorporated into a traditional Hindu world view, without diminishing many of its starkly irrational, occult and pseudo-scientific tendencies.

II

Let me illustrate what I mean by the superficial and schizophrenic nature of Indian modernity. I reproduce here an excerpt from a short essay titled 'Is India a Science Superpower?' I wrote for *Frontline* (September 10, 2005):

> The next century belongs to India, which will become a unique intellectual powerhouse …capturing all its glory which it had in millennia gone by", Dr Raghunath Mashelkar, the director general of India's Council of Scientific and Industrial Research declared in *Science* earlier this year. Thomas Friedman, the *New York Times* columnist and author of the recent bestseller, *The World is Flat*, agrees that India, with its talented yet low-cost brainpower, is on its way to becoming the "innovation hub" of the global economy. Not to be outdone, the British weekly *New Scientist*, has dubbed India the world's emerging "knowledge superpower"…
>
> …What does not make sense, however, is the radical disconnect between the dreams of becoming a science superpower, and the grim reality of the mind-numbing superstitions and life-threatening pseudo-sciences that are thriving at all levels of the Indian society. Indian scientists may well be the most sought-after workers in the global economy, but many behave as if what they do inside their laboratories has nothing do with the supernatural and/or spiritual "truths" that pass as "scientific" explanations of natural phenomena in the rest of the society…..

Do I exaggerate? Here is a report on the six weeks I spent in north India this summer:

> In early May, throughout the countryside in northern India, thousands of children, mere girls and boys, were married off on Akshay Tritya, a day considered astrologically auspicious for marriages and other new ventures. The rare social worker who tried to prevent child marriages had her hands chopped off by those bent on defending their hoary traditions. There are, of course, many complex social and economic reasons why child marriages still persist in India in significant numbers. But these secular motives come with full blessings of our priests and astrologers who have declared the bright sun and the moon on the third day of the month of May to be auspicious for new ventures, including child marriages which are supposed to bring good karma to the parents of child-brides.

Meanwhile, astrology was getting a corporate makeover to appeal to the "modern", urban middle classes, who were being bombarded with advertisements by the World Gold Council to celebrate the "auspicious" alignment of the stars by buying some more gold jewellery.

If you thought that scientists, especially space scientists, would have something to say regarding the astrological logic underlying popular traditions (old and new), well, think again. While the country was gearing up for *Akshay Tritiya*, India's top space scientists were busy seeking the blessings of Lord Balaji at the Tirupati temple for a safe launch of the polar satellite launch vehicle. A miniature model of the rocket was laid in the *sanctum sanctorum* of the temple and prayed over by priests in the presence of 15 scientists, led by the space-agency chief, Dr G Madhavan Nair. Scientists, who have not let go their own security blanket of gods, can hardly be expected to question the comforting but false illusions astrologers sell to ordinary people.

Meanwhile, the many satellites that India's space agency has launched in the past were busy beaming TV programmes selling wild, unsubstantiated health benefits of yoga and Ayurveda, delivered in a heady brew of spiritualism and Hindu nationalism. India's most popular tele-yogi, Swami Ramdev, has amassed a fortune selling his Divya yoga on the TV. Interspersed with the swami's calls for awakening "*desh ka svabhiman*" (national self-respect) by teaching "*crore saal purana vigyan*" (science dating back 10 million years), one finds totally unsubstantiated claims about the power of yogic postures, deep breathing and his own Ayurvedic concoctions for every ailment known to humankind including cancer, heart disease, diabetes, glaucoma, obesity…

What is remarkable is that all these reason and evidence defying traditions come wrapped in the fancy dress of "science". On my visit to Chandigarh, my hometown, I heard an Arya Samaj preacher exhort the devotees at an open-air public discourse held right outside my house (with loudspeakers set at full blast) to "read the ancient Vedas to learn all the sciences known to humanity".

(He was discoursing on how to succeed in the modern world with its prized high-tech jobs!) Astrology, yogic ideas of *prana* and *kundalini* and even the ideas of reincarnation, karma and *varna* (i.e., caste order) are justified in the language of modern physics and evolutionary biology. All these ancient metaphysical speculations are proclaimed to be "Vedic sciences" (i e, empirically testable and logical within the metaphysics of the Vedas) and they are supposed to have been belatedly rediscovered by modern science. What we have here is pseudo-science in its purest form, that is, religious dogma, lacking rigorous scientific evidence and plausibility, dressed up as science...

Everything Vedic is "scientific" and every "science" known to human kind only affirms the wisdom of the Vedas. Indeed, claims of the "innate" scientific temper of the Vedas occupy a place of pride in the Hindutva assertions of Hindu superiority over Islam and Christianity, which are declared to be merely faith-based "creeds". Science, "vedically" interpreted, is feeding into Hindu chauvinism.

III

That "the Vedas" are conflated with science as we know it today will hardly come as news to anyone who knows anything about India. This is routine business and has been going on since the very introduction of modern science and technology in India, dating back to the 18th century. (Indian rationalists, in comparison, have never enjoyed the same degree of cultural hegemony. The marginalisation of rationalism in India's cultural politics is a topic for another day and another essay.)

Most Indians pause to think about this streak of scientism in modern Hinduism,[2] just about as much as fish pause to reflect upon the water they live in which is not much at all. It has become a part of the commonsense of modern, science-educated, English-speaking Indians to treat the teachings of popular gurus, yogis and swamis as vaguely "scientific", and therefore modern. Indian scientists, for the most part, have not challenged the religious uses of science: they tend to keep their laboratory lives and their personal lives in separate water-tight compartments. Our public intellectuals and social critics, meanwhile, have been more exercised about the real and imagined scientism of the modern Indian state, than about the scientism that pervades modern Hinduism.

I believe that we need to pay closer attention to Hindu scientism because it is a symptom of the deeper cultural contradictions that afflict India's modernity. We pride ourselves in being modern, yet we trample upon the first principle of modernity, namely, to draw principled distinctions between science and metaphysics, or between verifiable knowledge of tangible material entities occupying space and time, and the intuitive knowledge of intangible soul-stuff god, brahman or any form of "subtle" spiritual energy that is not accessible to the five senses all human beings share alike. The *sapere aude* spirit that Kant was talking about meant just this: to divest metaphysicians, theologians and priests from making existence claims about supernatural powers, and conversely, using existence claims of natural sciences to affirm supernatural or spiritual powers. The point of the Enlightenment project was not to destroy religion, but to limit what it could say about nature and how it could use the authority of nature to defend its dogmas.

Modernity in India lacks the spirit of *sapere aude*, understood as setting limits on the authority of religion, as separating the realms of science and religion in the larger culture. If anything, India has followed an exactly opposite path, absorbing more and more of science into the traditional teachings of the Veda, Vedanta, Yoga Sutras and Ayurveda. Indeed, as I will argue below, India has taken a uniquely "inclusive" (read co-optive) route to the classic phenomenon of counter-Enlightenment or reactionary modernism.[3]

IV

In order to understand India's unique style of counter-Enlightenment, we must first be clear what we mean by the Enlightenment. Without getting entangled in the many nuances of the European Enlightenment, we can keep three general propositions in mind.

To being with, the Enlightenment refers to a historical epoch which began with the English Revolution in 1688 and culminated in the American Declaration of Independence in 1776 and the French Revolution in 1789. There was no one unified movement called "the Enlightenment" that swept through all of Europe simultaneously. There were, rather, a series of debates and critiques directed against the authority of inherited intellectual and religious traditions. These debates took different shapes and forms in different national contexts, affecting all of western Europe and northern America to a lesser or greater extent. In all cases, these movements were supported by the rising class of the industrial bourgeoisie. In Protestant England and America, the Enlightenment took place largely in alliance with the church, while in largely Catholic France, the church was relatively less hospitable to new ideas. Led by a new class of intellectuals who made a living by writing for the "grub street" (newspapers, periodicals and cheap novels) and by giving lectures and demonstrations on current sciences in coffee houses and pubs, Enlightenment ideas found a receptive audience among the reading public.[4]

Secondly, for all the national differences, the movements included in the rubric of the Enlightenment were marked by, to quote Alan Kors, the editor of a new Encyclopedia of the Enlightenment, "an increasingly critical attitude toward inherited authority,…a sense that armed with new methods and new powers, the human mind could re-examine claims upon it…including the claims of religion. This was not a rejection of authority per se, but of arbitrary authority whose sole claim upon one's mind or body was its having withstood the test of time".[5] *Sapere aude* "dare to know" was the motivating force behind the entire movement, and was used by British freethinkers as their rallying cry much in advance of Kant.[6]

Third and finally, notwithstanding all the postmodernist attacks, it is still possible to defend the Enlightenment as the precondition for any kind of progressive politics. As Stephen Bronner writes in his spirited new book, *Reclaiming the Enlightenment,* nearly all aspects of modern life, especially "the ideals of personal autonomy, tolerance, secularism and reason, developed against the backdrop of Enlightenment's protest against the exercise of arbitrary power, the force of custom and ingrained prejudice [that] justified social misery".[7] On this reading, it was the Enlightenment that made real the ideals of modernity that were only latent in the Renaissance, the Reformation and the Scientific Revolution. Enlightenment, then, is considered by many intellectual historians as the true beginning of modernity.

V

Against this background, let us return to Kant's motto. Why did he make *sapere aude* "the courage to use your own reason" the distinguishing mark of his times? After all, the Age of Enlightenment was hardly the first to apply the power of reason to comprehend nature and society. Human beings in all societies and in all epochs have exercised the powers of observation, logic, and experimentation, along with imagination, insight, myth and magic to understand and materially manipulate the force of nature. What was so special about reason in the Age of Enlightenment that Kant would turn it into a rallying cry for freedom?

While the philosophers of the Enlightenment exhorted their fellow citizens to live by the light of reason, they were simultaneously redefining reason by setting limits on what can legitimately be known, given the kind of sensory apparatus and reasoning powers human beings are endowed with. The philosophers and architects of the age of reason, from Locke and Hume in England; to Voltaire, Diderot and Montesquieu in France; Kant, Lessing and later Marx in Germany; and Jefferson, Paine and Franklin in the US, were impressed by the success of the Scientific Revolution, especially the disciplined empiricism of Newton. His famous laws of force and universal gravitation emerged out of patient and careful observation of comets, planets, objects in motion and transmission of light. Newton, in other words, derived his first principles from the empirical investigation of phenomena. This, to the philosophers of the Enlightenment, was in refreshing contrast to the method of theologians and metaphysicians who started with infallible, divine revelations and proceeded to deduce the knowledge of physical phenomena from them. They recognised full well that Newton's observations themselves required metaphysical grounding, that is, a belief in the existence of order created by god. But what they found remarkable was that Newton used this metaphysical belief as a springboard for empirical examination, rather than as an *a priori* truth to explain material phenomena.

Newton's method became the paradigm of reason for the Age of Enlightenment. The philosophers denied most strenuously that it was possible to make any factual claims about the world based upon "pure reason" by which they meant Gnostic intuition, mysticism, "direct realisation" or revelation, that is, any means of knowing which cannot be validated by sensory experience. Only those objects in the "phenomenal world" (to use Kant's vocabulary) that correspond to human categories of space, time and causality can possibly become objects of our experience, and human knowledge can only extend to these objects. We have no possible way of knowing the objects of the "noumenal world" (to use Kant's vocabulary again), the things-in-themselves that lie outside our mental categories of space, time and causality. This meant that supra-sensible entities like god, absolute consciousness, soul, vital spirit, etc., which lack extension in space and time, forever lie outside human abilities to know them. We can therefore make no empirical claims about this supra-sensible or noumenal world, neither can we use our knowledge of the noumenal reality to explain the phenomenal world.[8] This world view did not exactly deny the existence of supernatural forces or ultimate realities, but it limited them to the world of noumena, totally beyond the reach of human experience. Such forces could be accepted as allegories, as poetry, even as necessary fictions to defend our moral intuitions about good and evil, but they could not provide foundations for knowledge of the natural world.

This was a monumental change. So far human history, science, or natural philosophy, had existed within the limits of religion. Henceforth, religion could exist only within the limits of scientific reason. This was the philosophical core of the Enlightenment, the rallying cry of the "moderns" against the "ancients".

This transformation had far-reaching consequences, not just for the conduct of science, but for the evolution of a democratic and secular public sphere. As the new historiography inspired by the path-breaking work of Jurgen Habermas has established,[9] the empiricist revolution in the conception of reason was hugely important in the creation of new ideals of publicness, open in principle (though not in practice) to all, in which all authority was open to critical scrutiny on the basis of evidence accessible to ordinary human faculties of sensory perception and elementary logic. Gradually, the old taboos which derived their force from natural law, which was supposed to express divine will, lost their powers to persuade. Depending upon the historical balance of forces between the church and the throne, and the allegiance and strength of the bourgeoisie who derived their wealth from industry and commerce, different degrees of secularisation took place in different societies, a process which is still in progress.

VI

Just as surely as day is followed by night, the Enlightenment was followed by the counter-Enlightenment. The proclamation of the autonomy and authority of testable, sensory knowledge, over and against revelations, mystical intuitions, miracles and all forms of extra-sensory knowledge was resisted by the keepers of faith everywhere.[10]

There are primarily two routes the counter-Enlightenment has taken through history: the less-travelled path of outright refusal, favoured by the orthodox observant communities, and the more popular and politically-correct option of co-option through indigenising or relativising the norms of reason, favoured by religious/cultural nationalists on the one hand, and the postmodernists and multiculturalists, on the other.[11]

The great refusal can be seen in the enclaves of traditionalism and orthodoxy in some heradim Jewish communities in Israel and the US, the Amish and among the separatist sects of evangelical Christians in the US. But this option of "just saying no" to the larger secular culture is becoming rarer and harder to maintain in the world increasingly permeated by modern technologies and new ideas.[12]

Cultural relativism, that is, not an outright refusal but a reinterpretation of the norms of empirical science within one's own civilisational or national culture, has been the preferred mode of most of the illiberal, counter-Enlightenment movements, notably the fascist movements in Germany and Japan in the 20th century, down to the religious fundamentalisms of the 21st century. Assorted fascists, Christian and Islamic fundamentalists and our own Hindu nationalists cannot be categorised as old-fashioned anti-modernists who want to take their societies back to some primitive pre-modern, pre-scientific age of faith and/or magic, insulated from global developments in science and technology.

They are more properly described as "reactionary modernists", a term coined by Jeffery Herf in his 1984 intellectual history of the Weimar and Nazi Germany. Reactionary modernists, in contrast to backward-looking golden-age pastoralists, say "yes" to modern technology, but "no" to the Enlightenment norms of scientific reason. They succeed in "mixing a robust modernity and an affirmative stance toward progress with dreams of the past: a highly technological romanticism".[13] Reactionary modernists, in other words, display a great enthusiasm for technological modernisation, overlaid with a deep aversion to rationalism, secularism and individualism that comes with modernisation. They want the fruits of modernisation, without the pain and joys of cultural dislocations that modernity brings.

The question before all reactionary modernists is how to use the technological products of modern science, while rejecting its world view and its norms of reason. The solution has been to remove scientific reason from the world view of the Enlightenment, a world view of reason, intellect, internationalism, materialism and redefine it in the jargon of authenticity, community, and heritage. The claims of science and modernity are not rejected out of hand, but "only" translated into an ethno-scientific vocabulary. Universalism of science is not denied in favour of anything goes kind of relativism, but modern science is deemed to be only one of the many other equally universalisable ways of knowing. The importance of subjecting beliefs to experience and evidence is not denied, but what constitutes evidence and experience is made relative to the metaphysical categories of the rest of the culture. While something called "science" is celebrated, it invariably ends up re-affirming and legitimising the traditional common sense of the culture, derived largely from the dominant religious tradition.

VII

Translating the empiricist tradition of modern science into the jargon of mysticism derived from Patanjli's Yoga Sutras and monistic strains of Vedanta has been the hallmark of neo-Hindu counter-Enlightenment. Declaring the Vedas to be based upon "direct realisation" of "higher realities", and therefore "another name for science", was the work of the thinkers of the Hindu renaissance, notable among them being the Adyar theosophists, Swami Vivekananda, Sri Aurobindo and Servapalli Radhakrishnan. Contemporary descendents of these 19th-early 20th century Vedas-as-science thinkers include the many monks of Ramakrishna missions around the world, "Vedic creationists" of Krishna Consciousness and well-known personalities like Maharishi Mahesh Yogi and Deepak Chopra and their many clones and/or admirers in the west as well as in India. The saffronisation of history, including the history of science, that we experienced under the reign of the Sangh parivar was a political expression of this long-standing conflation of the Vedas with modern science.

Like other reactionary modernists before them, neo-Hindu philosophers seem to accept the challenge of the Enlightenment. They accept that with the success of the scientific revolution, as Radhakrishnan put it in his *Hindu View of Life*, "the centre of gravity in religion has shifted from authority to reason". But, and here is the rub, they define the non-sensory, intuitive or mystical experience, the so-called "pure reason", to be actually referring to real, causal entities and/or energies which can be directly "seen", or "heard" by altering your consciousness through yoga: mystical insight is interpreted as an empirical experience of natural order. They argued that what the yogis experienced "in here" in their minds actually corresponded with realities "out there", and by experimenting with their inner selves, Vedic adepts can come to know and control external reality. Indeed, neo-Hindu and Hindutva writings are replete with references to the Vedas as describing empirical facts and laws of nature that were actually "seen" and "heard" by the mythic authors of the Vedas through the process of yogic meditation alone.[14]

In other words, while neo-Hindu philosophers accepted the Kantian emphasis on using "one's own reason" and not the authority of priests and holy books, they rejected the limit the empiricists had put on the powers of reason. The empiricist tradition that flowered during the Enlightenment had steadfastly denied that one can make any substantive claims about reality based upon "pure" or non-sensory reason alone. Neo-Hindu philosophers insisted that within the holistic world view of Vedanta, in which consciousness permeates all matter, non-sensory, meditative knowledge of one's inner self can give you insights about the ultimate reality of the material world. While the Enlightenment drew a line between sensory and non-sensory perception, neo-Hindus rejected this line and insisted that mystical experience constituted a valid empirical experience.

How was this interpretation of mysticism as providing valid empirical knowledge defended? Here we find striking similarities with the postmodern theories of all knowledge including modern science as being paradigm-bound, a construct of specific metaphysical assumptions, which serve the interests of power over nature and society. Neo-Hindu thinkers have asserted that the Kantian restriction on sensory knowledge as the only legitimate source of knowledge is a construct of the dualist world view of Abrahamic or "Semitic monotheistic" religions in which god/divine consciousness is separated from brute matter. Because the Hindu tradition does not separate matter from spirit but considers all matter living and non-living as the embodiment of "vital energy" ('prana') or consciousness ('brahman'), it is considered perfectly legitimate within the Hindu tradition to treat mystical "realisation" of the spirit in our own selves to correspond to the spirit, or essence, of the rest of the universe. And, Vedic science apologists go on to insist that because a "reductionist" materialist-empiricism is an aberration of the Abrahamic faiths, anyone who accepts its validity suffers from "mental colonisation" and trying to semitise Hindu dharma.[15] This defence of mystical empiricism, unfortunately, got a big boost from the idealistic interpretations of quantum mechanics popularised by Fritjof Capra, Mahesh Yogi, Deepak Chopra and Amit Goswami in recent years.

So, how modern are we, really? If modernity means a differentiation and separation between science and religion, between sensory experience and the mystical experience of metaphysical "realities", we in India have a long way to go. Rather than challenge the authority of private mystical experiences of our "holy" men and women with the evidence and logic that is available to ordinary men and women in everyday walks of life, we have dignified mystagogy with the name of "holistic science". We have been playing word games, rationalising and pretending we-know-it-all while, in fact, we do not.

VIII

But one can sympathise with all that I have said above and still ask: So what? What is so terribly wrong with the scientism of neo-Hindu gurus, intellectuals and believers? By presenting ancient wisdom in scientific terms, are they not encouraging Indians to study science and develop a scientific temper? By refusing to separate consciousness from matter, are they not avoiding the sterile materialism of the west? Besides, why crusade against superstitions anyway? Isn't it true that irrationality can coexist with good science as, say, in America, the world's undisputed leader in science? Others advise that as long as you have secular institutions and laws in place, popular superstitions are not worth worrying about. Still others insist that rather than fight "mere" ideas in people's heads, we should fight for a socially just society: secularisation, they say, will naturally follow the lead of political and economic reforms.

I do not deny that there are specks of truth in most of these caveats. One cannot simply reason a just and secular society into existence; scientific temper alone can only take you some distance. A rationalist offensive against superstition and pseudo-sciences can only be meaningful if it is a part of a larger political movement that can meet people's aspirations for existential security and justice in this life, rather than in some future birth, in some future 'sata-yuga'. I agree that it is not people who need to be made more rational, but that social systems that thwart rationality and creativity need to change.

I even grant that at least initially, under colonialism, Hindu scientism did serve a useful purpose: it gave us the much-needed confidence to confront colonial stereotypes of irrational and mystical India, and it made the pursuit of science sufficiently non-threatening. But over time, Hindu scientism has morphed into a full-blown pseudo-science with nationalistic overtones. There are relatively harmless but self-indulgent New Age-ish aspects of the mind-matter holism that are becoming increasingly popular among the urban sophisticates in India: a bit of yoga here, some vastu there, with Ayurvedic potions thrown in for good measure. But this is the same world view which also justifies the traditional logic of innate karmic purity and hierarchy, and which legitimates the paranormal "spiritual" powers of god-men and soothsayers. I understand that some kind of superstitious thinking will always be with us: that is perhaps an unavoidable consequence of the human imperative to find explanations, right or wrong. Granted, also, that there is no need to declare a war on every idea that does not meet the standards of scientific justification, for human beings do not live by reason alone. But as long as superstitions and pseudo-sciences enjoy the kind of cultural hegemony, patronage and linkages with nationalism as they do in contemporary India, they remain a political force to reckon with. In view of their pervasive social influence, they cannot be treated as matters of personal belief.

It is sometimes argued that rationalisation and secularisation of world views will follow, pretty much on their own, in the wake of technological and economic modernisation, and therefore no special engagement with the content of people's beliefs is needed. Indeed, even well-meaning secularists are weary of criticising religious beliefs as elitist and disrespectful of ordinary people. But there is no evidence that modernisation of infrastructure and economic relations alone, or by itself, can bring about a secularisation of beliefs. Beliefs, especially those beliefs that answer our existential questions regarding death and birth, misfortune and good fortune, right and wrong, have a life of their own. Beliefs don't simply lie down and die when the social context changes: instead, they mutate, and adapt to the new social context. The planetary configuration of Akshay Tritiya, to take an example cited above, did not cease to be auspicious for modern Indians, many of whom have grown rich on jobs in the high-technology and scientific research and development. Rather, it is mutating from a day that was considered auspicious for child marriages into a day that is auspicious for conspicuous consumption of gold jewellery. But the underlying idea that stars can confer auspiciousness on human actions remains intact. India today is witnessing a resurgence of many old superstitions and rituals couched in pseudo-scientific language to appeal to modern sensibilities. Economic and technological modernisation, then, is no guarantee of a secular culture. The creation of a secular culture requires active engagement with the religious common sense of the people.

It is also true, as some scientist friends have suggested, that good science can exist and even thrive in otherwise superstitious societies. It is true that modern science has become relatively autonomous of the larger culture. It has developed a naturalistic metaphysics and an empiricist methodology of its own which is often at odds with how the workings of nature are interpreted in the rest of the culture. It is possible for scientists trained in the culture of their own arcane specialisation to do great science, without ever having to engage with the religious interpretations of nature that prevail outside the walls of the lab. The two cultures simply don't seem to talk the same language, even though they, in fact, often offer competing explanations for the same phenomena (e.g., Darwin's evolution by natural selection, and "spiritual evolution" as propagated by "integral yoga" of Sri Aurobindo and his followers, or the "Vedic creationism" through the agency of karma and rebirth, as propounded by the followers of Krishna Consciousness).

But, while science can thrive in otherwise irrational societies, there is a huge price to pay for the gap. It is not a coincidence, in my opinion, that a majority of Americans who believe in divine creation over Darwinian evolution should have believed the Bush administration's completely bogus case linking Iraq with terrorism: in both cases, there is a faith-based, rather than evidence-driven, reasoning at work. In both societies, there is a need for scientists to stand up for critical reasoning and sound evidence both inside and outside the laboratory. The need to speak up for, defend and advocate scientific temper is far greater in India where superstitions and pseudo-sciences have a far deeper hold on the popular psyche and where they often make a difference between life and death, between dignity and indignity of caste and other hierarchies.

To conclude, Indian modernity will remain incomplete and schizophrenic until the time it is animated by the spirit of critical reasoning. Kant's motto: *sapere aude!* "Have courage to use your own reason!" remains as vital for India today as it was in his own time. Special pleas to spiritualise nature and science in the name of Vedic holism may make us feel superior over other faiths and cultures, but it will not help us shed our own prejudices and superstitions.

Notes

* This is a much revised version of the paper that appeared in *Eastern Quarterly*, Vol. 3, Issue II, July-August 2005, pp.75–85. A Hindi translation, by Om Prakash, has appeared in *Pahal*, 84, November 2006.

1 In modern Hinduism, "the Vedas" have come to mean a loose, miscellaneous category of texts which refer not only to the four canonical Sanskrit Vedas, but to all kinds of post-Vedic, extra-Vedic and even anti-Vedic texts. Neo-Hindu gurus and intellectuals have honed the tradition of claiming Vedic origin of, or at least Vedic parallels with, any idea that they find useful for perpetuating an essentially spirit-based and hierarchical cosmology of the Vedas and Vedanta. For a hilarious (but misleading and dangerous) example, see Deepak Chopra's bestseller, *Quantum Healing*, Bantam Books, New York, 1989, where he puts a spin of quantum physics on developments in neurosciences as if they were merely re-stating the spiritual truths known to Vedic rishis.

2 By scientism, as it appears in religious apologetics, I mean the positivist belief that if religion is to be made respectable and meaningful, it must be "scientific", that is, its metaphysics and epistemology must meet the standards of empirical testability that apply in modern science. This leads to recasting traditional metaphysics in scientific-sounding theories. Rather than use the empirical methodology of modern science to challenge metaphysics, and create a non-metaphysical, non-supernatural basis for religiosity as was the intent of logical positivists and empiricists scientism in the hands of religious apologists turns modern science into a vehicle of traditional metaphysics. Hindus are not alone: American Protestantism also has strong strains of scientism. For a comparison, see 'Secularisation without Secularism?' in my *The Wrongs of the Religious Right: Reflections on Science, Secularism and Hindutva*, Three Essays Collective, New Delhi, 2005.

3 Here I continue the dialogue I began regarding the place of science in Indian culture in my earlier work, notably, in *Prophets Facing Backward: Postmodernism, Science and Hindu Nationalism*, Permanent Black, New Delhi, 2004, and my more recent 'Response to my Critics', *Social Epistemology*, Vol. 19, no. 1, 2005, 147–91.

4 Dorinda Outram, *The Enlightenment*, Cambridge University Press, Cambridge, UK, 1995.

5 Alan Kors, Preface, *The Encyclopedia of the Enlightenment*, Vol. 1, Oxford University Press, New York, 2003.

6 For a fascinating study of the Enlightenment in Britain, see Roy Porter, *The Creation of the Modern World: The Untold Story of the British Enlightenment*, WW Norton, London, 2000.

7 Stephen Eric Bronner, *Reclaiming the Enlightenment*, Columbia University Press, New York, p.7.

8 While Kant provided a defence of empiricism against the radical scepticism of Hume, he also limited empirical knowledge to the phenomenal world only and denied the possibility that we will ever know if empirical knowledge of phenomena corresponds to the structures of the real world, the world-in-itself. As Kant himself admitted, he had set limits on science to make room for faith. Ernst Cassirer's classic *The Philosophy of the Enlightenment*, Princeton University Press, Princeton, NJ, 1951, is still one of the best explorations of the implications of Kantian philosophy for the Enlightenment.

9 Jurgen Habermas, *Structural Transformation of the Public Sphere*, MIT Press, Cambridge, 1989.

10 Isaiah Berlin's writings remain the best starting point for understanding the opposition to the Enlightenment. See Isaiah Berlin, 'The Counter-Enlightenment' in *The Dictionary of the History of Ideas*, Vol. II, Charles Scribner's Sons, New York, 1973.

11 I have shown the overlap between Hindu nationalist and postcolonial views on science in my earlier writings. See note 3.

12 See Martin Marty and Scott Appleby, *The Glory and the Power: The Fundamentalist Challenge to the Modern World*, Beacon Press, Boston, 1992 for a good description of the enclaves of orthodoxy.

13 Jeffery Herf, *Reactionary Modernism: Technology, Culture and Politics in Weimar and the Third Reich*, Cambridge University Press, Cambridge, 1984.

14 For a classic statement of yoga as a source of knowledge and control of the natural world, see Vivekananda's exposition of Patanjli's Yoga Sutra in his well known lectures on raj yoga. Critical reflections on this kind of "spiritual empiricism" are few and far between. But see Willhelm Halbfass, 'The Concept of Experience' in *India and Europe: An Essay in Understanding*, SUNY Press, Albany, 1988 and Anantanand Rambachan, *The Limits of Scripture: Vivekananda's Interpretation of the Vedas*, University of Hawaii Press, Honolulu, 1994. For a stinging critique of treating mystic experience as having ontological references, see Agehananda Bharati, *The Light at the Centre: Context and Pretext of Modern Mysticism*, Ross Erikson Publishers, Santa Barbara, 1982.

15 I have been at the receiving end of these kinds of slurs from Hindutva supporters.